PRAISE FOR
RELATIONSHIP GOALS

"The way God has moved this message like wildfire to millions of people speaks volumes about its value. There is no turnkey or quick fix to having rich relationships. With down-to-earth honesty, Michael Todd not only gives you a vision for what your relationships could look like, but he also gives you the road map to get you there. I'm confident that no matter where you are and no matter what stage of life you are in, *Relationship Goals* will be a game changer."

—LEVI LUSKO, lead pastor of Fresh Life Church
and bestselling author

"Michael Todd is one of my favorite preachers. He is a great man of God. I am so proud of him, and I am so glad he wrote this much-needed book about relationships. I know you'll love his authentic, personal, and engaging way of explaining how relationships work best when we do them God's way. Using principles from God's Word, this book will help you learn how to have better and more intimate relationships with your friends, your spouse, and, most important, with God!"

—ROBERT MORRIS, founding lead senior pastor
of Gateway Church and bestselling author of *The Blessed
Life, Beyond Blessed,* and *Take the Day Off*

"We are often encouraged to practice what we preach. However, I think it's also important to preach what we practice. This is exactly what Mike and Natalie Todd have done. They have taken their lumps and transformed them into lessons. They have taken their pain and turned it into purpose. They have taken their mistakes and turned them into ministry. They have taken their blessings and turned them into a book. If you are looking for a blueprint to a blessed relationship, this book is for you."

—DR. DHARIUS DANIELS, lead pastor of Change Church and author of *Relational Intelligence*

"Mike has been a dear friend since we were twenty years old—just recording music in Tulsa together. As we've both moved into ministry, I've seen God expand Mike's reach greatly, but his humility and kindness have never changed with all the public praise. He's the real deal on and off the stage, and he's such an exemplary man of God for our generation. The message God has given Mike on relationship goals is one hundred percent fire! It is so important for anyone wanting to build Christ-centered, successful relationships. I'm so thankful for Mike and Natalie not just sharing a message but sharing their lives as a great example for marriage and family!"

—PAUL DAUGHERTY, lead pastor of Victory in Tulsa, Oklahoma

RELATIONSHIP GOALS

RELATIONSHIP GOALS

HOW TO WIN
AT **DATING, MARRIAGE,**
AND **SEX**

MICHAEL TODD

with Eric Stanford

WATERBROOK

Details in some anecdotes and stories have been changed to protect the identities of the persons involved.

Hardcover ISBN 978-0-593-19257-3
eBook ISBN 978-0-593-19258-0

Cover design by Kristopher K. Orr; cover photography by Graceson Todd; chapter 1 photographs courtesy of the author's personal archives

Published in the United States by WaterBrook, an imprint of Random House, a division of Penguin Random House LLC.

WATERBROOK® and its deer colophon are registered trademarks of Penguin Random House LLC.

The Cataloging-in-Publication Data is on file with the Library of Congress.

Printed in the United States of America
2020—First Edition

8 9 7

SPECIAL SALES
Most WaterBrook books are available at special quantity discounts when purchased in bulk by corporations, organizations, and special-interest groups. Custom imprinting or excerpting can also be done to fit special needs. For information, please email specialmarketscms@penguinrandomhouse.com.

Hardcover ISBN 978-0-593-19257-3
eBook ISBN 978-0-593-19258-0

Published in the United States by WaterBrook, an imprint of Random House, a division of Penguin Random House LLC.

WATERBROOK® and its deer colophon are registered trademarks of Penguin Random House LLC.

The Cataloging-in-Publication Data is on file with the Library of Congress.

Printed in the United States of America
2020—First Edition

8 9 7

SPECIAL SALES
Most WaterBrook books are available at special quantity discounts when purchased in bulk by corporations, organizations, and special-interest groups. Custom imprinting or excerpting can also be done to fit special needs. For information, please email specialmarketscms@penguinrandomhouse.com.

RELATIONSHIP
GOALS

HOW TO WIN
AT **DATING, MARRIAGE,**
AND **SEX**

MICHAEL TODD

with Eric Stanford

WATERBROOK

I would not know anything about relationship if it weren't for my beautiful wife, Natalie. She gave me the grace to grow from a boy into a man, a husband and a father, her pastor and her best friend. I'm sharpened daily by her passion to cultivate our family into what God has called it to be, and I'm eternally grateful to God for trusting me with her.

Nat, out of the entire human race, you truly are my ultimate relationship goal.

CONTENTS

RELATIONSHIP GOALS

1 TAKING AIM

God's plan, God's plan
I can't do this on my own
—DRAKE, "God's Plan"

#RelationshipGoals has been a trending topic worldwide for years now. Search for this hashtag on social media, and you'll find celebrity couples posing at exclusive clubs, stills from romantic movies at the point where the boy gets the girl, cute couples kissing on a beach or cuddled up in bed, a boyfriend-girlfriend pair holding balloons in the park and giving the impression that their relationship has never been anything but pure happiness. And when people repost these pictures with the hashtag, what are they saying? They're saying, "I want a relationship like that!" Kim and Kanye, Jay and Bey, Prince William and Kate, Will and Jada, some unidentified couple who look really good in a picture that happened to go viral—we can easily become obsessed with their seemingly perfect images and make them our idols and ideals.

Okay, maybe you've never noticed the #Relationship Goals tag online, much less posted anything with it. But if I were to ask you to think about the relationship you want, would an idealized picture flash into your mind? Maybe it's you with a tall, handsome pro athlete who takes you on shopping sprees. Or maybe it's you beside a girl who's hood like Cardi B but has a sweet side like Carrie Underwood. Is he an amazing listener with a classic swag like George Clooney and a job that pays both his bills and yours? Can she cook like your mama and get just as hype as you do when your team scores?

Now, if you just asked *What's wrong with that?* in your head, allow me to submit to you that maybe there's more to relationship than what pop culture has taught us or our own imaginings have dreamed up. Maybe our society sells an illusion of intimate relationship that's more like a mirage—the closer you get to it, the more you realize it's not real at all. Maybe the things we tend to celebrate are built on unstable foundations and are bound to eventually fall. But also . . . maybe there are some truths here that can be unlocked about how and why human connection is so important and how we can achieve it.

> THERE'S MORE TO RELATIONSHIP THAN WHAT POP CULTURE HAS TAUGHT US OR OUR OWN IMAGININGS HAVE DREAMED UP.

I believe so, and that's why I've written *Relationship Goals* . . . about *real* relationship goals.

WHY OUR GENERATION IS SO CLUELESS

Let me rewind really quick through some of the photos of my life so you can get to know me, okay?

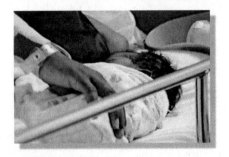

There's baby Mikey in his crib, born 1986 in Tulsa, Oklahoma. Ain't he cute?

Here's one of me and my whole family when I was little: Mom and Dad with their four *really* active boys, minus my baby brother, Graceson, who came unexpectedly late. How could they do it with all of us and still be married today, after forty years? I don't even know.

Now, here I am playing drums at church, the place where I spent most of my childhood. So, I *knew* what was right from an early age; I only wish I'd *done* what was right more often.

There's me on tour with the late, great Wayman Tisdale, thinking I'm going to be the next Tony Royster Jr. (Look him up. He's awesome.)

This here is a picture of the most beautiful girl in the world the night we met, but I'll get to her in a little bit.

There's me at Edison High School, where I became the first African American "Mr. Edison"—an achievement that came as a surprise to many but was the start of my being recognized as a leader. After high school, I had six months of high-quality education from Tulsa Community College. (No picture needed for that.)

Then I started a business of my own. So, here's me at So FLY (Sold Out Free Life Youth) youth and young adults ministry, where I began teaching in ministry and discovered through a lot of crazy situations that the book you're holding *had* to be written.

And here is a very influential person in my life: Bishop Gary McIntosh, my ministry mentor and the man who gave me opportunities to preach. Then, in 2015, he entrusted me with leadership of the church he'd founded: Greenwood Christian Center, now known as Transformation Church.

This one is of me up on stage, doing what I was created to do—re-presenting God's Word.

So, that's it—no, wait. Let me rewind some more, because I want to show you something I skipped over. Okay, there it is: a picture of me when I was in kindergarten. I don't have a shot of the actual moment, but it was about this time that I had my first kiss. That's right, in kindergarten! I purposely built a wall out of blocks during free-play time; then I asked a girl named Sierra to come behind the wall with me, where we wouldn't be seen by the others. When she did, I kissed her straight on the lips. (Sierra, if you're reading this, I hereby apologize.) My excuse is, I was only five. Girls were already fascinating to me; I just didn't know what to do with them.

That little trip down Michael Todd Memory Lane reminded me of something crazy—in all that time, nobody ever really explained relationships to me. I grew up in church but never heard much about the biblical model of right relationship. There was the granddaddy of all rules (can you guess it?): "Don't have sex until you get married. Period." That was the main message preached to me about romantic relationships. Then there was the less emphasized but probably just as important "Get friends who aren't bad influences." Aaand yeah, that's about it. Not very extensive, huh? I'm pretty sure you've heard those rules, too, but have you ever heard anyone explain how to follow them or why you should follow them?

As a matter of fact, when most people think about relationships, they do not think about church or Christians as a source of wisdom at all. It's sad. But if we're honest, we can admit that many believers have failed at relationships, so we don't have as many great examples to model after as we should. Far too many saved, sanctified, Sunday school–lovin', stompin' and clappin' saints die lonely, and far too many preachers travel the world for ministry but have failed marriages and no real friends. It's no secret that the church hasn't done a great job at confronting real-life issues, so many of us didn't have much choice but to allow movies, TV shows, each big cousin who had a new girlfriend every Thanksgiving, and the slew of instafamous people who take great filtered photos to become our relationship gurus.

If you're anything like me, I'm willing to bet Cory and To-panga (from *Boy Meets World*) taught you more about romantic relationships than your youth pastor did. I might be dating myself (shout-out to all the '80s babies!), but I must admit, watching the Fresh Prince of Bel-Air make a fool out of himself chasing after any girl—"Baby, I know your feet must be tired, 'cause you been runnin' through my mind aaall day"—started to shape my idea of what pursuit was supposed to look like. At the same time, watching Martin and Gina (from *Martin*) argue was carving out my context for normal communication.

Let me warn you, some of the things you'll read in this book are not usually said in books by Christian pastors. I believe in discovering the truth by uncovering lies, so we're going to put the realities of today's relationships up against the truths in God's Word about how to live with others. The Bible, in fact, is the greatest source for relationship wisdom, and it's time we start applying it to relationships as they really exist. In the One who made us and knows us, there's hope for better relationships for people like me who grew up clueless.

IT'S TIME WE STARTED APPLYING IT TO RELATIONSHIPS AS THEY REALLY EXIST.

But then, maybe your experience was the opposite of most and you did see healthy relationships all around you, live and in person. Even so, maybe you never could figure out how the gears fit together to make that beautiful antique clock work for you. Perhaps the perceived perfection of somebody else's relationship has put unhealthy pressure and expectations on you and now you feel an anxious desire to rush the process. I'm here to let you know that there's hope for you too.

Some may subscribe to the belief that there's no point in even trying to have a successful, healthy relationship, and I can't say I blame them when it seems all we see are statistics like the sky-high divorce rate and the countless celebrity break-ups recorded in tabloids. The saddest truth is that these same trends are just about as prevalent in the church. Many supposedly Jesus-loving people think it's normal and fine that many people have had more sexual relationships than they've had cars (and you know you get a new one of those every few years). That's what happens when pursuing "good times" dating, instead of faithful marriage in covenant, is your default.

Now, don't get me wrong—I'm not here to judge (cue Tupac's "Only God Can Judge Me"). I'm here to try to help. I believe that God has given me a playbook and a platform to help each and every one of us *win in relationships*. It doesn't matter if your current status is single, married, dating, divorced, courting, looking, waiting, thirsty, stalker, player, or it's complicated. And it's not just about romantic relationships either, though we're going to emphasize that side. Wouldn't you like principles you could use in relationships with your sis, your nana, your boss, your bro, your BFF, and every other person you're in close relationship with?

We're about to embark on a relationship roller coaster, and trust me, this is not a book you want to put down midride. I believe God is going to give wisdom and revelation through the pages you're about to read, and it's going to transform your relational life.

But first, you should have some quality assurance that when I'm saying something to you, God has already taken me through the wringer on this. So, let's go back to the most beautiful girl in the world I was telling you about.

MY PROMISE: I'LL KEEP IT 100 PERCENT

I met my future wife, Natalie, at a mutual friend's birthday party on December 14, 2001, at a rec center. I was fifteen. She was fourteen. She walked into the place with long black hair and a black dress, and I said, "What?!" I'd never seen anything so exotic and beautiful.

I promised to myself, *She's gonna notice me tonight.* I proceeded to act a plum fool. I did everything I could to make myself seem interesting. I bragged. I tried to make her laugh. I showed her my dance moves. At fifteen, I thought I had the tightest game in the world—but the truth was, I was scared it wouldn't be enough to get me this gorgeous girl.

As I was about to leave the party, I was thinking about

how to go back over to Natalie, across the room, and say goodbye. Right then, she came and found *me*! "Where's my hug?" she said. "Don't I get a hug?" That hug, to me, was like somebody giving me the biggest kiss in the world.

From that point on, we dated for about eight years, except for a ten-month period of insanity (more on that in a future chapter). Thank God, we got back together. We got married in a huge wedding in 2010. Now, out of our love, we have three awesome kids: Isabella, Michael Jr. ("MJ"), and Ava.

I know that to some people Natalie's and my finding each other so early and getting married at a young age might seem like an ideal they missed out on or like we couldn't relate to them. But even if it was quicker than for some people, we've been through the whole relational process, and we've made and learned from plenty of mistakes along the way. We're not perfect, but we're progressing. I promise in this book I'll share authentically from my pain and mistakes and I'll keep it 100 percent.

Also, as a pastor I've had hundreds of people come to me with their stories of problems in dating, sexuality and self-control, relationships with girlfriends/boyfriends, baby mamas/baby daddies, husbands/wives, and more. With their permission, I'll share some of their stories, changing their names to protect their privacy but telling the straight stuff about what they went through.

WE HAVE MORE RELATIONSHIPS AND LESS LOVE, MORE SEX AND LESS INTIMACY.

We live in a world that has more and more relationships and less and less love, more and more sex and less and less intimacy. When I think about the pain I've experienced and have seen others experience from bad relationships, I can't wait to share with you what the Bible says about how to do relationships so that you can minimize the pain and start to benefit from the rewards. To do that, you've got to have a goal.

SIXTH-GRADE BOYS DON'T HAVE AIM

A *goal* is the result or achievement toward which effort is directed. Take away the goal, and what good is the effort? Imagine an archer with a bow and arrow. If he doesn't have a bull's-eye target, he can aim and shoot if he wants, but the arrow is not going to hit anything purposeful. So, what's the point?

I've noticed that one of the key issues that hinders people from reaching their relationship goals is the fact that they don't know how to aim. It reminds me of the time when the planning committee at my middle school had the bright idea to install urinals on the wall of the second-floor boys' bathroom. I'll just say, there were clearly a lot of goals, but there wasn't enough aim.

I'm sure you can imagine the rest of that scene. A lot of messes had to be cleaned up, and it left a nasty situation for other people to walk into. It also lowered the standard for everyone else. I'm sure the thirty-ninth boy who walked into that restroom took one look, shrugged, and thought, *What's the point in aiming?*

This scenario looks a lot like our society's perception of relationships; most people see them as messy and stained with a lingering aroma that tells where people have been and how badly they've missed the mark. When the damage is done, attitudes have formed, innocence has been stolen, and questions begin to flood our minds. *Is love even real? Does anyone's relationship last longer than a few months? What's the point in aiming at these goals?*

The truth is, having a goal without aim is senseless, but having a goal without God is pointless.

Many of us don't have our aim directed when it comes to relationships. We take whatever comes. We do whatever's comfortable. But we don't really know where we're going or why.

> IN RELATIONSHIPS, WE DON'T REALLY KNOW WHERE WE'RE GOING OR WHY.

Don't believe me? Have you ever known a girl who dated pretty much any guy who happened to show an interest in her, without ever stopping to think about the kind of guy who would really be right for her? Or a couple who have dated for a long time and have gotten so comfortable with it that they aren't making any move toward marriage? Or a married couple who have let their former passion turn into a business partnership for child rearing and home maintenance?

Don't feel like I'm trying to pick on you or lock you into something. I don't know you well enough to do that. Truth is, biblical principles are unchanging, but we're at different places and we can have a variety of relationship goals within the guardrails that God has set up. So, relax and remember . . . you don't have to have your whole life figured out from the start. Your relationship goals can, and actually should, change over time. You aren't doomed if you've made a mistake; every one of us has access to heavenly redemption. I should know.

What I am asking is, What is your goal? And what I'm suggesting is for you to align your goal with God's goals for relationships. Set the target and sure up your aim so that the relationship arrow of your life doesn't go astray.

RIP UP YOUR LIST

So, maybe you're the kind of person who somehow has never gotten around to making conscious relationship goals and has just fallen into the relationship ruts. But more than likely you've got some kind of goals, targets, or markers of success in mind when it comes to relationships. That's better. Still, even if you do have targets, I want you to be open minded about whether these are the *right* targets. You might need to reexamine them. Because, see, it's possible to have a target for your arrow that's the *wrong* target.

Let's say you're single and ready to mingle and you've made a list of things you want in a significant other. One could be "He's got to be at least this tall and make this much money" or "She's got to have the cute face and a tiny waist." This shows that most of our lists tend to be a little (or a lot) superficial and might reflect not what we actually need in a partner but more of just what we want at the time. I assure you, life has a way of changing, modifying, and redefining what success in relationship looks like for all of us.

LIFE HAS A WAY OF REDEFINING WHAT SUCCESS IN RELATIONSHIP LOOKS LIKE FOR US.

When I'm going on a road trip, I usually tell my phone where I want to go, and it gives me directions on how to get there. But success for the journey happens only if I've given my phone the right destination. Let's say I've planned to take my family on vacation to Disney World in Florida, but I get careless and accidentally say to my phone, "Grand Canyon." Then I just mindlessly follow the directions electronically spoken to me by my phone. Do you think I'll arrive at the correct destination? Of course not. My kids will be looking for Mickey Mouse, but all they'll see is a bunch of dusty rocks. On top of that, I can guarantee there will be disappointment, frustrated expectations, wasted resources, and lost time.

My point is, many of us are tapping in our own destinations for relationships, but they are not necessarily the goals that we should really be pursuing. We should follow a plan (directions) that will get us to the goal (destination) that we actually want to reach.

Let's be honest—many of us make plans that fail, even though they seemed really good at the time.

> There is a path before each person that seems right,
> but it ends in death. (Proverbs 14:12)

I've seen that verse proved true so many times—that everything that seems right isn't always right. And someone else who is learning the same lesson is a young woman named Sarah.

When I met Sarah not long ago and talked to her about her relational life, she was kind of down. She was still single past the age when she'd hoped to get married.

"Would you say that you have a clear idea of the kind of guy you want?" I asked, trying to be helpful.

"Oh yeah. And I'm starting to think that's the problem."

Years earlier, Sarah had developed a lengthy list of requirements for any guy she dated. I tried to keep a straight face while she ran through them for me. I'll just share a few with you . . .

- come from a two-parent home (That eliminates about a third of the population right there.)
- be a successful business owner (Notice: not just have a job but own a major business.)
- be a preacher or work in ministry (A successful business-man *and* a preacher?)
- be able to tell jokes that make her laugh
- be very athletic

After years of refusing to get to know men or let them get to know her because they didn't line up with her criteria, she was starting to wonder if her list was a bit unrealistic. *Yeah, girl. Maybe just a little.*

It's good to take aim at relationship goals. That's a whole lot better than just passively letting society or the media or our family experience teach us how to do relationships. But we also have to make sure we have the right goals, ones that will contribute to the life we ought to be leading. For that, we have to go to the source of meaning.

GOD'S PLAN

I believe the beauty of life is being a part of something that is way bigger than yourself. It's God's plan.

I know you may think that your plan is pretty awesome, but what if a plan was made for you before you were even born? Yeah, I like that: God's plan was made for you *before you*! Let me prove it.

Once, God told the prophet Jeremiah,

Before you were born I set you apart
    and appointed you as my prophet to the nations.
      (Jeremiah 1:5)

In other words, Jeremiah had a God-given mission before he even took his first breath. But before you dismiss that as a special case, let me tell you that it's not just prophets or other unusual people who have a place in God's plan. We *all* have God-given, inborn purposes.

An apostle said it: "We are God's masterpiece. He has created us anew in Christ Jesus, so we can do the good things he planned for us long ago" (Ephesians 2:10). You're a *masterpiece*! He's got *good things* for you to do, planned before you were born!

I'm going to be talking a lot about purpose in this book. We all have a variety of purposes in life that I truly believe we're supposed to fulfill. These aren't just things we dream up. They're dreams that God has planted in us. And my purposes added to your purposes, added to the purposes of millions of others, combine to produce the kingdom that God is building. Within that perspective, what seems small (my little dreams and aspirations or yours) is really big.

So, we should look at this purpose thing in a context—the context of what God is doing. What is God's purpose in relationships? What guidelines has He been teaching about relationships that we need to follow so that we're doing this His way?

Our encouragement is this: It's not all on us. God instructs us, guides us, and teaches us how to aim at the right relationship goals.

I will instruct you and teach you in the way you should go;
I will guide you with My eye. (Psalm 32:8, NKJV)

GOD WILL HELP US FIND THE RIGHT TARGET FOR OUR RELATIONAL ARROWS.

The more we seek Him, the more we'll find out what He wants for us and the more we'll desire to pursue it. God will help us find the right target for our relational arrows. And it will be better than we could find anywhere else.

Culture's views on relationship are a moving target. Culture says marriage looks like this in one decade, then like that in another decade. The term *dating* used to imply physically going out somewhere. But now we have "Netflix and chill," and you don't have to be committed to anybody to cross the line into private areas.

God wants every single one of us to have successful relationships, but we have to have a goal that is stable enough for us to aim at. So, let me point out to you that the only thing that is unchangeable, unwavering, and immovable is the Word of God. Isaiah 40:8 tells us, "The grass withers and the flowers fade, but the word of our God stands forever." So, I dare you—no, I double-dog dare you—to let the standard of your relationships be God's Word, even if it's just for the time it takes you to finish this book. Let's just see what would happen in our hearts, minds, and lives if we would follow the stable, biblical model of relationships instead of following our own feelings or other people's examples.

MY TARGETS, YOUR TARGETS, OTHER TARGETS

As you speculate about relationship goals for yourself, the temptation will be for you to compare what you need and want in relationships to everyone else's needs and wants. But remember this: we all have different targets. Your age, stage, experiences, and place in life are unique to you. I challenge you to take some time to really think about your individuality and your special calling in life as you're praying and thinking about what you're going to aim for in your relationships.

Just to suggest the diversity that's possible, here are some relationship goal examples:

- "I need to break up with my abusive boyfriend, move out of his apartment, and spend some time not dating anybody. I need to rediscover who I am and focus on getting back to God."
- "I'm so used to being in multiple relationships for fun, but I'm tired of empty relationships. I want a relationship with depth."
- "I want to find a wife who is cool with a lot of travel and a small income because I am committed to a career as a musician in a band."
- "I want to get to the point where I can forgive and reconcile with my dad so that my kids and I can have some kind of relationship with him before he passes."
- "I want to be free of my addiction to porn and start living in the real world instead of a fantasy world inside my head. I've failed at this before, and I know I need God to help me."
- "My new company is big. I'd really like to find a few coworkers here who are believers like me."
- "I've prided myself on being independent, but lately I'm realizing my need for companionship and community."
- "My sponsor says my sobriety is at risk if I keep hanging around with friends who are drinkers. I want some new people to hang out with who know how to have fun without a glass in their hands."
- "I really want to get engaged, but I have so many fears and so many memories of past failures. I need the courage to ask my girlfriend to marry me and begin to lead her boldly in Christ."

- "I want to find a junior partner who shares my values and whom I can confidently give my business to when I retire."
- "I've been the cause of so much hurt in other people's lives that I feel like I don't deserve good relationships. But I want to try again."
- "I know I'm only a teenager and haven't had a serious relationship yet, but I really feel God is calling me to be a mom of several children. I need to start getting wisdom to prepare for that future."
- "Our separation was a mistake. I think she feels it as much as I do. I know the kids do. I want to explore with her how we can reconcile and try again, with God in the middle of our marriage this time."
- "I never had the example of godly parents, so I want to start learning what that means before this baby is born."

So, where are *you* in your relational journey? Are you starting to sense new relationship goals forming in your mind or heart? If you quiet the loud cries of culture, you might just hear the Holy Spirit start whispering to you. That's my prayer for you.

> IF YOU QUIET THE CRIES OF CULTURE, YOU MIGHT HEAR THE HOLY SPIRIT WHISPERING.

HOW TO WIN IN RELATIONSHIPS

How much time do we spend pursuing relationships that would be a mistake if we ever got them, trying to make bad relationships work better, or healing from past relationships that blew up on us? From the perspective of a pastor whom hurting people tell their stories to, I can assure you, it's a huge amount of time!

Wouldn't it be better if we put our energy into having the best possible relationships in the first place? It's not a perfect world, we're not perfect people, and no relationship on earth is ever going to be perfect. But God has given us the Bible and the church to help us win in relationship. He helps us find the right targets and straightens our aim.

You don't have to listen to me if you don't want to. You can go ahead and secretly envy what other people's relationships are like (or what you *think* they are like). Or you can make up your own goals based on selfish and probably unrealistic desires. But do that and you'll keep getting the kinds of results that you've already been getting: heartache, disconnection, disappointment. Am I right?

Or you can take aim at new relationship goals that will help you fulfill your purposes in life and keep you in line with God's eternal truths. I don't care how old you are, how many relationships you've had, or what your current relationship status is—you *can* do relationships differently. You just need the right goals, ones that will enable you to get a W.

God is the real, ultimate, and total winner in this universe. If you're with Him, you'll be a winner too. Set your relationship goals in partnership with God and in keeping with His teaching, and you'll find fulfillment—not just in the relationships themselves but in your whole life.

PROGRESSION, NOT PERFECTION. I told you earlier that my relationship with Natalie, my wife, is not perfect, but it is progressing. *Progression, not perfection*—that's a phrase we throw around a lot in our church, and I believe it's appropriate for you, too, as you look at forming new relationship goals. There's pressure here, but it's the pressure to get started; it's *not* the pressure to get everything right all at once.

You can win at relationships. I don't care what your Christian walk looks like or even if you aren't sure you really believe. If you're sprinting, jogging, or barely stumbling ahead, keep moving forward. I believe God will get you to the place you're supposed to be. He'll do it because He loves you and because, whatever else might be going on in your relational life, He is faithful in His relationship with you.

I believe you can win at relationships. Now *you* believe it.

2 BEFORE THE PERSON

You say I am held when I am falling short
When I don't belong, oh You say I am Yours

—LAUREN DAIGLE, "You Say"

Before there was ever a person on this earth—and in fact before there was even an earth—there was already relationship. How's that? It's because God the Father, God the Son, and God the Holy Spirit existed as three persons in one. Now, I can't totally explain the Trinity. Nobody can. It's real, but how it works is beyond our ability to comprehend. The thing is, the Bible makes it clear that the three persons of the Trinity have dwelled together *forever.*

Meaning relationship was, is, and forever will be. Cool, huh?

Maybe the coolest thing about all this (for us anyway) is that humanity was created out of that everlasting relationship. The Trinity had a conversation and agreed, "Let us make human beings in our image" (Genesis 1:26). The Trinity didn't need us. They were already perfect, complete, and fulfilled within Themselves. But out of the overflow of Their love, They decided to create humans, both male and female.

The first human, Adam, lived in the Garden of Eden with God as his companion from his first day. In other words, he had a relationship with God before there was even one other human to know. The picture we get in Genesis 2–3 is that

God and Adam were homeys. They would hang together in the garden, talk about this and that, and take walks to look at the shiny new plants and animals while enjoying the cool evening breeze together. All by themselves, just the two of them.

Here's what we need to get out of this: No matter what other relationships we have (or don't have), all of us can have a relationship with God. Through Christ, He invites us into the same kind of connection He has within the Trinity—a loving, giving relationship. Even though the top relationship goal we have on our minds right now probably is finding or improving a human relationship, it's important to see how our relationship with God should come

WHEN WE PUT GOD FIRST, HE'LL BLESS THE REST.

first and above all other relationships. It's *the* relationship, our ultimate relationship, and all blessings flow out of that relationship. In fact, one of those blessings is that He enables us to do our other relationships at their highest possible level. When we put God first, He'll bless the rest.

THE HIDDEN CONNECTION

May I make it very plain for you? You can't have the best kind of relationships—you can't win at relationships—without God. Whether it's a friendship, a sibling relationship, a romantic relationship, or whatever it is, it can be pretty good in its own way, and you can come up with great Instagram posts. But when you cut that thing wide open, there are two people who need a Savior. You might have an emotional connection or an intellectual connection or just a strong physical connection, but without God that connection isn't enough.

I'll speak about myself here: Godly relationships are about sacrificing for others, showing kindness, having integrity, forgiving one another, and all kinds of other tough stuff like that. To really do those things, I need Jesus. It just doesn't come naturally to me. Me without the Lord? I'd suck. I mean, I have a nasty attitude. I cut people off. I will completely check out.

But honestly, that's all of us, right? Your issues may be different from mine, but wouldn't you have to admit that without God, you're a hot mess too?

I think this is a part of where Jesus was going with Matthew 22:37–38: " 'You must love the LORD your God with all your heart, all your soul, and all your mind.' This is the first and greatest commandment." All of us have things that are really important to us, like our careers, our families, our spouses. I'm really into the time I spend with my wife and kids, my preaching, and my music. For you, sports or making videos or—for all I know—selling homemade dog costumes on Etsy may be a really big deal. But no matter what, God is saying, "I need Me to be first because I know how to supply everything else in your life."

Jesus went on to say, "A second [commandment] is equally important: 'Love your neighbor as yourself' " (verse 39). We're going to come back to this verse in the next chapter, but right now I just want you to see the connection between the two commandments. Jesus picks one from Deuteronomy and one from Leviticus and puts them together. One, two—love God and love others. The best human relationships flow out of relationship with God.

I'm not saying that people who are living far from God can't sometimes have good relationships. Obviously, they can and do. But I'm saying that on the spiritual level at least, there's a difference. If you and I don't have our constant source as God, we will always be deficient and not able to give all the grace, give all the peace we should in relationship. We won't be able to walk in the love of Christ like we're supposed to.

> **IF WE DON'T HAVE A CONSTANT SOURCE IN GOD, WE WILL ALWAYS BE DEFICIENT.**

This hits close to home for me because I've seen the direct impact of someone's decline in his relationship with God creating a decline in all his other relationships.

TRAIN WRECK

Doug was one of our family's good friends. I've known him and his wife since I was born. Birthday parties, Christmases, all the scrapbook things you could think of—Doug was a part of that. I got an inside look at how their family thrived in fun, business, faith, and generosity, even to the point of adopting other children into their home and transforming their lives.

Unfortunately, something happened that shook Doug's faith. He became more pessimistic, judgmental, isolated, and selfish. He was no longer devoted to the pillars that got him to a place of thriving—things like prayer, reading the Word, and community. Eventually Doug's faith grew so thin that he decided to no longer believe in God. That decision changed everything. His business partnerships failed. His friendships dwindled. His children were damaged. And his marriage ended in divorce.

The Bible says, "God has made everything beautiful for its own time. He has planted eternity in the human heart, but even so, people cannot see the whole scope of God's work from be-

NO ONE IS EXEMPT FROM NEEDING A RELATIONSHIP WITH GOD. ginning to end" (Ecclesiastes 3:11). There's a part of us made to connect with the eternal glory and beauty of God. And when God put eternity in the human heart, He knew we would need to depend on a relationship with Him to understand it all.

Nobody can convince me that what happened to Doug wasn't a direct result of his broken connection with God. I saw it going on with my own eyes. It was like watching a slow train wreck. As soon as he lost relationship with God, all his other relationships suffered. It's a reminder to me—and now to you—that no one is exempt from needing a relationship with God.

THE RELATIONSHIP GIVER

Let's go back to creation. God made the sun and the moon and the sky and said, "It is good." He made water and dry land and said, "It is good." He made plants like spinach and kale and then, for me, all the ingredients for a delicious soul-food dinner and said, "It is good." Then He made the sea creatures like Willy and Nemo and Flounder and all the wild animals like Timon, Pumbaa, and Simba, and He said, "It's good." When He made Adam, He said, "It's very good." It was all good.

But pretty soon God said for the first time, "It's not good." It's not that God had messed up—He never messes up. Something was missing. "The LORD God said, 'It is not good for the man to be alone'" (Genesis 2:18).

This principle is true for all Adam's children as well. It's not good for you to be alone. It's not good for me to be alone. When we set up a life that is guarded and gated, the Enemy comes to attack us. When we're isolated, we're at more risk of listening to lies about who we are and coming to believe them as truth. We all need relationship with people who can remind us of the truth and dispel the falsehood, who can show us some of the love our hearts need, who can help us along our way. God knows this. And that's why God wants relationship for us.

WHEN WE SET UP A LIFE THAT IS GUARDED AND GATED, THE ENEMY COMES TO ATTACK US.

Is it hard for you to believe that a major part of God's plan for your life involves relationship? He wants you to have healthy and successful relationships—yes, you, the one who is content working from home and taking online courses, does all your shopping on Amazon, and doesn't like going to church because everyone always wants to hug you and the preacher enjoys making you turn to your neighbor to say something random. God created you to be in relationship with others, even if you're introverted, you're shy, you've been hurt before . . . or you're just kinda over the whole "needing other people" thing. And it's a good thing too.

Have the courage to say, "God wants relationship for me!"

He wants you to have a best friend, even though the last one stabbed you in the back. He wants you to have pastors and mentors who create a safe place to grow and become. He wants you to be in a marriage that works and is marked by love, honor, respect, and fun. Granted, your past relation-ships might have been, well . . . the opposite of that. But God is a redeemer, so He can take whatever is broken and jacked up and work it for your good.

With God leading, relationships are a good thing, the solu-tion to the problem of aloneness. Ecclesiastes 4:9–12 says,

> Two people are better off than one, for they can help each other succeed. If one person falls, the other can reach out and help. But someone who falls alone is in real trouble. Likewise, two people lying close together can keep each other warm. But how can one be warm alone? A person standing alone can be attacked and defeated, but two can stand back-to-back and conquer.

You can usually tell whether a relationship is from God just by looking at this one qualification: *Does this relation-ship help me?* Think through all your close relationships and ask yourself that question about each one.

We tend to tolerate so many relationships that are taking away from us—stealing our peace, ravaging our joy, and keeping us up worrying at night. Why?

You might say, "But they're my friends and they're so fly."

Okay, but if they're *so fake,* you need to let them go. If the people around you are keeping you stuck in your chains, it doesn't take divine intervention or a miraculous sign from God to reveal to you that those relationships aren't helping you.

Many of us have experienced poisonous relationships in some way or other, and it may have negatively affected our desire to ever have human connection at all. Let me encour-age you: don't allow the pain from your past relationships to make you forfeit your future ones.

Don't be like Bobby Boucher's mama from one of my favorite '90s movies, *The Waterboy*. She was so afraid of everything that she called everything "da debbil" (aka "the devil"). "School is da debbil!" "Foosball is da debbil!" "Girls are da debbil!"

Relationships are not "da debbil," but if they're not handled God's way, they can open the door to "da debbil." Many relationships have been misused just because we didn't understand the God-given purpose of them.

THE RIGHT PERSON FOR THE PURPOSE

There's something else we need to notice from the Garden of Eden story: God gave Adam a job. "The LORD God placed the man in the Garden of Eden to tend and watch over it" (Genesis 2:15). Adam was supposed to manage paradise (not a bad gig, if you ask me).

So, Adam not only had relationship before he had a person; he also had a purpose before he had a person. God gave him work to do before He gave him a wife. (And by the way, this is not just about men. Rebekah was carrying water when she heard about Isaac. Ruth was working in the field when she met Boaz.)

When planning to create Eve for Adam, God said, "I will make a helper who is just right for him" (verse 18). Eve aced the Ecclesiastes 4 litmus test of being a partner who helped. And what did she help Adam with? One big thing was that she supported him in doing his God-given job. She helped him fulfill his purpose.

See, people are so often trying to get a person without first understanding their own purpose—or at least without taking

> A CLOSE RELATIONSHIP IS GOING TO HAVE A HUGE IMPACT ON HOW WELL YOU FULFILL YOUR PURPOSE.

it into account. But a close relationship is going to have a huge impact on how well you can fulfill your purpose. This is true with your BFF, your college adviser, your roommate, your business investor . . . and especially your spouse.

This isn't about being selfish—"I want a spouse who will free me up to do whatever I want." No, no, it's about finding a partner who will help you to fulfill the purpose for which God put you on this earth instead of getting in the way of that. (And of course you need to be the kind of person who does the same thing for your spouse, because she has a purpose too.) This is a big deal. It's about following God.

However much you know about your purpose (I'm about to help you with that) and whatever it might be, remember that Adam started working in his purpose before he ever got a person. What I'm saying to you is that while you're looking for somebody to date, someone to marry, or a new friend in the town you just moved to, you can be working on your relationship with God and working on doing what He's called you to do.

When that person who gets your purpose and believes in it and loves you finally comes along, he'll fit right into your life. The right spouse will help you move further along the path God lays out for you, not try to hold you back from that path.

A cool example of this idea of relationships pushing toward purpose is my parents.

Typically, when a couple are in ministry, the man is out

HOPE FOR THE FUTURE

Maybe you've been dating, dating, dating, but it's never gotten to the point where somebody took a knee and said, "Will you marry me?" Maybe you made a mistake or somebody took advantage of you, and there's a baby but no relationship. Or you went through the whole romantic process and it seemed like you were living the dream, but instead of happily ever after, the process was cut off with another stage you didn't see coming: divorce.

I feel you. The world's not perfect like it was in the Garden of Eden. But I know this: God can heal. God can redeem. God can put us back on track and bring good things out of a bad situation. Don't lose your faith in the possibility of a loving, supportive, productive relationship. And don't forget that God still loves you, has things for you to do, and has blessings with your name on it.

"I know the plans I have for you," says the LORD. "They are plans for good and not for disaster, to give you a future and a hope." (JEREMIAH 29:11)

front leading while the woman is in more of a support role. This was completely flipped with my parents. I watched my mom sing, preach, and pray for people all over the world in a leadership role while my dad ran sound, carried bags, and managed her itinerary in the background. It was my dad's humility as a "man's man" to support my mother that allowed them to have such a great impact. He helped push her into purpose, and she did the same for him.

After decades of my dad being secure in the shadows, my

mom encouraged him that his wisdom was valuable. Now he leads others as a pastor and counselor on the same platforms that he once supported her on.

Just like my parents, there are right people for your unique purpose. The right friends. The right partners. The right teammates. And the right spouse. Before you find that right person, you have to find your purpose. The right person is on the other side of the right purpose.

FIND YOUR PURPOSE

How do you know what kind of purpose you have for your life? First of all, you don't know it all perfectly at first. You begin sensing it, and God reveals more as you go.

I had no idea that God wanted me to be lead pastor of Transformation Church. But back when I was a teenager, I began sensing that God wanted to use me in His work. I got involved in my church. People started affirming the gifts they saw in me. I was given chances to lead—and I wasn't very good at it at first, but there was some promise. Over time, I was given more and more responsibility and I began to develop into the leader I am today. Not perfect, but progressing.

That's how it works. God reveals purpose bit by bit.

Also, your purpose can change from season to season. It evolves. It grows. Sometimes it comes to its natural end. Or it may lie dormant.

There's a lot I still don't know about why God has me on this earth and what He wants to do through me. One reason I know this is that some of my inborn desires are still unfulfilled. And you, I'm sure, have a lot to learn still about your purpose as well. My encouragement is, if you have a relationship with God and you're really trying to draw near to Him, He will reveal things to you.

Now, sometimes the process of learning and growing and moving toward our purposes isn't easy. Maybe you hate your job, but God is saying,

> IF YOU HAVE A RELATIONSHIP WITH GOD, HE WILL REVEAL THINGS TO YOU.

"I know you only make ten dollars an hour, but there's something about this job I'm using to reveal who I've called you to be." You've got to be patient and open.

At times I've thought, *Why am I here?* The only thing I could conclude was *If I'm here and it's uncomfortable, it's for my growth. God is trying to show purpose in my life.*

You might be in a place like that right now. Accept the training, remind yourself it's not forever, and keep your spirit tuned in to God's Spirit.

One other thing: *relationship itself* is a purpose. God gives you friends so you can build into their lives and they can build into yours. Getting married is a lifetime commitment that will be rewarding but also costly to you at times. Just don't go looking for others to give you what only God can—your purpose. Look only to God for that. And trust Him to bring people into your life who can push you ahead and whom you can push ahead in His plans.

CLOSER TO GOD

As a young man, I made the most life-altering decision. It wasn't the college I'd go to or even whom I'd marry. It was inviting the Lord Jesus Christ to become my Savior. I haven't been perfect, but that one act of faith has transformed my life.

And if I'm being honest, I hope you make that same decision for yourself. It's so easy. According to Romans 10:9, all you have to do is "declare with your mouth, 'Jesus is Lord,' and believe in your heart that God raised him from the dead, [and] you will be saved" (NIV). If you want to take a minute to do that right now, I promise it'll be the best decision you've ever made. And if you're still not sure, it's okay. I believe that at just the right time, you'll know what to do.

Once we become a follower of Jesus, that all-important relationship exists . . . forever! What we do from that point on is *cultivate* the relationship.

Adam was a cultivator. He cultivated the garden. Eventually he would cultivate his relationship with Eve. He also cultivated his relationship with God by taking advantage of opportunities to talk and interact with the Lord.

So that's why I'm saying we, too, should be cultivating our relationship with the Lord. Every day. Wherever we are in relationship to God, we can move forward to know Him more clearly, love Him more deeply, and obey Him more faithfully.

WE SHOULD BE CULTIVATING OUR RELATIONSHIP WITH THE LORD. EVERY DAY.

Maybe you're exploring this whole faith thing and this idea of cultivating a relationship with God seems a little intimidating. Well, my boy James gives us some advice and a promise: "Come close to God, and God will come close to you" (James 4:8). It's just that simple. You take a step, and you become more aware of how close God is. While you're cultivating your relationship with God from your side, He's doing even more to cultivate it from His side.

For you, what does this require?

You need to have a daily devotional life. I'm not going to tell you how to do that or when or for how long, but somehow you've got to crack that Bible open or scroll on that app every day. I promise it'll make you better. It's the only book where you read it and *it reads you*.

And you need to pray. That's simply talking to God. "God, I'm frustrated about this traffic that I'm stuck in right now. I just need You to help me not cuss these people out." God's not mad at that. Even down to the deep things like "I'm insecure about my future." He just wants you to talk to Him, and He'll speak back to you.

And then you need times of worship. Worship is expressing our love to God through our lives. One of the best ways to express worship is to play music that magnifies God and minimizes our doubts, anxiety, fear, and frustration.

At different seasons of life, your time with God might look different. If you're single, you may have a lot of time to really invest in learning about and experiencing God. So, go for it. Do intensive studying on your own, attend Bible college, go to conferences, or live out your faith on a mission trip. Being engaged is a time to establish habits of praying together as a couple and talking about faith, encouraging each other. This is also a great time to establish community with other couples who are going the same way. When you're married, you're going to want to make attending church together a habit and figure out how your quiet time fits in to your schedule together. The thing is, wherever you're at, you keep your priority but you adjust.

The parenting years can be tough on a devotional life. Natalie and I have three kids, so quiet and solitude are hard to come by nowadays. We've realized either we're gonna have to wake up early or we're gonna have to stay up once the kids have gone to bed in order to meet with the Lord. So, we do it. We each also take a private spiritual retreat once a year.

Your season of life may have to dictate how you go about pursuing God, but as long as you do it, it's going to be so beneficial, the basis for winning in other areas of your life. I'm convinced God has to be the center of your life.

The rest of the book is about these human relationships. Before we get to some specific topics of human relationships, though, I want to put it all in context for you. I've already hinted at how it works—it's all about relational seasons.

ROMANTIC RELATIONSHIP PROGRESSION

If your childhood was similar to mine, you remember a song that used to be sung on playgrounds and with other children. It went something like this:

> Michael and Natalie sitting in a tree,
> K-I-S-S-I-N-G.
> First comes love, then comes marriage,
> then comes baby in the baby carriage.

For many of us, this song might have been the first time we heard an explanation of relational progression: love > marriage > baby. It's a little vague and incomplete, but it seems simple enough.

Then we grow up. And because we live in a fallen world and our society is backward and perverse, we realize that love > marriage > baby is not the progression in everybody's life. Just think about all the different scenarios. Sometimes it's baby first. Then because you had a baby, you decide you might as well get married. And since you are married, "Lord, could You please help me to love her?" Or sometimes it's love, and then there's a baby, and then we're not too sure how much we can trust each other so maybe we'll get married or maybe we won't. From what I see on TV and online, it almost seems like a competition is going on to see who can have the most creative out-of-alignment relationships.

I want to help you understand there is a God way of progressing in relationship. It has more parts than just love, marriage, and baby and results not in confused, failed relationships but in successful, productive relationships made of two people who are healthy in themselves. These are the kind of people we have just been looking at—people who have a relationship with God and are trying to help each other do His will. It might take a while to get this process ingrained in our minds in place of all the other approaches that culture gives us. But the Bible says God can renew our minds and transform us (Romans 12:2), and we can trust Him to do that in this area for sure.

Singleness > Dating > Engagement > Marriage > Love > Children

First comes **singleness**. I know this is not a popular one. Not many people I know are happy to live without a bf/gf, much less a h/w. But, actually, singleness could be the most important time of your life because it's a prime time when God reveals to you who you are. You become self-aware. You find purpose. The future begins to come into focus. We've talked about how you have purpose before the person, and this is the phase when it happens.

Many marriages aren't whole because they have a lot of holes—secrets, pains, scars, fears, insecurities, and so on—that one partner is desperately hoping a spouse can fill. But what if each person had taken the time to heal and develop before they even met? Singleness is the time.

When you feel like you know yourself well enough and you're walking with God, the next step is **dating.** But I'm not talking about recreational dating—just going out with any-body who attracts you or because you want to have fun or because you're scared to be alone. If you do that, you give permission for anybody to walk in and out of your life. And then you end up putting yourself in a position to take your eyes off pleasing God. So, what I'm advocating is *intentional* dating—spending time with another in a God-honoring way to try to find out if that person is right for you.

If you find somebody who is walking with God and the two of you want to get married, there should be an **engage-ment.** That's the period of time when a couple are committed and planning toward their wedding, when they will enter into holy matrimony before God. It's a good time to talk deeply and develop plans and lay a groundwork for your future life together.

And then after engagement, there should be **marriage.** Marriage is different from hooking up or living together be-cause it is a covenant relationship. I call marriage a sex con-tainer because, in God's plan, it is the only relationship where sex should be taking place (and it should be taking place there *a lot*). Of course there's more to marriage than just sex. In fact, a marriage between a man and a woman who have godly relationship goals offers the best picture we have to understand the relationship between God and His beloved people.

After marriage there should be **love**. Why would I say love *after* marriage? Well, have you read 1 Corinthians 13? Because I don't know if you can truly do the type of stuff you have to do to really love somebody without sacrificing and giving up a lot for that person. I believe that you can like somebody a whole, whole bunch, but until you have to give to that person like Christ gave for the church—laid down His life in sacrifice—have you loved in the full manner?

And then out of our love in marriage we may reproduce, if God gives us that blessing. Having **children** is a little echo of the Trinity's saying, "Let us make human beings in our image." A married couple have a beautiful, reciprocating, complete love already between themselves, but out of the overflow of their love, they choose to produce new little human beings (diapers, teething, and 2:00 a.m. feedings included). And the relationship cycle starts again.

Every part of this process is good. Every part is appropriate. "For everything there is a season" (Ecclesiastes 3:1). So, hear me now: Whatever relational season you're in, don't just be in it. *Embrace it.*

This is what I like to hear:

- "I'm single, and I'm living my best life."
- "I'm dating, and I don't know yet if she's the one, but I'm loving what we've got right now."
- "We're engaged, and we can't wait to get married!"
- "We're married and falling more in love than ever."
- "We've got kids, and we can't believe how rich and full our life is."
- "The kids are grown and out of the house, but we still see them a lot. Meanwhile, we're rediscovering each other in this empty nest, and it's peaceful and warm, like a glow."

EMBRACE THE SEASON YOU'RE IN, THANK GOD FOR IT, AND MAKE THE MOST OF IT.

Embrace the season you're in, thank God for it, and make the most of it.

Remember, God wants you to have relationships. Healthy relationships. Rewarding relationships. Relationships that give you an opportunity to grow and serve and make a difference in the world.

If your relationship with Him is number one, He'll take you from wherever you are and move you on to where you need to go next.

3 THE S-WORD

I know I'm not alone

—ALAN WALKER, "Alone"

Now I'm feeling how I should
Never knew single could feel this good

—JASON DERULO, "Ridin' Solo"

We're now making our way through the relationship progression, and I want to start by addressing the s-word. Yup, that's right. *Single.*

Beyoncé made "Single Ladies" an anthem for all the women who are single, know they lookin' fine, and want to taunt the men from their past for making a mistake when they "should've put a ring on it." But if we're honest, usually when someone struts into a room and flaunts her single status, it's because she doesn't wanna be single!

I had a single young lady come up to me one time and say, "It just feels like it's time for me to be in a relationship."

"Why?" I asked.

"I've been single two years. I mean, that's a long time, Pastor Mike. It's just . . . it's just time."

I said, "I hear you that you want to be married. I believe that's going to happen for you—you're beautiful, you're talented, you're gifted. But right now, I feel like God's trying to supply you with some stuff you need. He's trying to re-create you and mold you. So, don't treat your singleness like it's a prison sentence you're serving."

Too many people I know are too eager to get out of singleness. When God said of Adam, "It is not good for the man to be alone," He didn't mean it's not good to be single. True, humans need to be involved in healthy relationships. In particular, nearly all of us crave to be intimate with someone else. But sex is not the only kind of intimacy, and marriage is not the only valuable season in our lifetime of relationships. The season of singleness is necessary—I'd dare say a priority—to anyone who wants to reach her relationship goals. Think about it: single was Adam's first relationship status.

If you're single, I'm sure many people and messages in this society have made you feel like you aren't enough without a significant other. The pressure to find a mate seems intense and unyielding, and you feel it from all sides. You didn't have a date to your best friend's wedding last spring, and he's been trying to fix you up with someone random ever since. People at your church whisper when you come around, "She's still single? What's wrong with her?" Your parents keep pressuring you to hurry up and marry someone because they want grandkids while they're still young enough to enjoy them.

All of that can make you start to feel like maybe somehow, in your single state, you are less than. Being single can start to feel shameful. Your life seems incomplete or even like a failure.

Worse, this kind of thinking can cloud your judgment until you find yourself rushing into relationships that don't suit you, settling on someone—*anyone*—just to satisfy others and calm your fears or address your libido. But these types of hasty decisions have serious consequences. Our high divorce rate may have less to do with bad marriages and more to do with bad singleness.

Let me encourage you with this: your singleness may actually be the most important part of the relationship process. It's not a curse. It's an opportunity! It's the best chance you'll ever have to work on being uniquely you—original and distinct. A good period of singleness means learning to be a unique self. God wants you to enjoy this season of life in which you can become whole and complete on your own, apart from a spouse or partner.

> **SINGLENESS MAY BE THE MOST IMPORTANT PART OF THE RELATIONSHIP PROCESS.**

If you are single, don't worry too much about dating and mating. That will come in its own time. Focus more on where you're at. Your current status lets you work on getting to know God better and worship Him. Singleness is a chance to understand yourself better, too, work on your weaknesses, build on your strengths, and move toward fulfilling the purposes God is planting in your heart. Along the way, you can clarify your relationship goals so that you'll be able to see it when the person comes along who is "just right" for you, as Eve was for Adam.

Even if you're not single, this chapter is for you because it demonstrates that you should always be working on yourself. Self-work is beneficial in all kinds of relationships. For example, the more you understand about yourself, the easier it is to have mature relationships with your parents or siblings. The more comfortable you are with you, the more people will be attracted to your authenticity and confidence. The more secure you are about your gifts, talents, and calling, the less you'll feel you have to prove.

The truth of the matter is that you are worth discovering. Nobody can do it for you, and nobody will make you do it, but everybody benefits from it.

THE GOOD, THE BAD, AND THE UGLY

In singleness, you get the opportunity to learn the good things about yourself—your love for travel, your desire to give back to your community, and your commitment to healthy living, for instance. But you also get to discover the bad things about yourself—like your overspending habits, your excessive desire for attention, and your fear of failure. No matter how ugly the process may get, like Anhayla's song says, "U Gotta Love Yourself" (U.G.L.Y.).

We looked at these verses in the previous chapter: "'You must love the LORD your God with all your heart, all your soul, and all your mind.' This is the first and greatest commandment. A second is equally important: 'Love your neighbor as yourself'" (Matthew 22:37–39). This shows us the connection between having a relationship with God and having relationships with people. But now let's look more closely at the second greatest commandment. Notice that it says, "Love your neighbor *as yourself*." Jesus drew a definite connection between our love for others and our love for ourselves.

According to the Word of God, there's a prerequisite for loving your neighbor: you can love your neighbor only at the level that you love yourself. Crazy, right? Most of us spend so much time hating things about ourselves that we don't realize we're crippling our ability to love others. There's no way you can figure out how to love somebody else well in a relationship if you have not first figured out how to love yourself in singleness.

{ **HATING THINGS ABOUT OURSELVES CRIPPLES OUR ABILITY TO LOVE OTHERS.**

Some of us treat ourselves so ugly: we settle for way less than what we know we deserve, we violate our bodies and our hearts and allow others to do the same, and we use our own words to put ourselves down constantly. If you devalue yourself, then you will inevitably end up treating your neighbor, or even your spouse, the same way.

To learn to love yourself the way God intended, you have to build a relationship with God, who *is* love. Remember, your relationship with Him is your ultimate relationship. But then loving yourself means accepting who God created you to be, as hard as that may be for you. It means taking the time to find your fulfillment in Him and realizing that only He can fill the emptiness you feel inside. Stop trying to fit other people into the God-shaped hole in your life.

We have a tendency to focus on loving our neighbor. But again, you can love your neighbor only at the level that you love yourself, and you can really love yourself only when you learn how much God loves you. Can I just pause for a moment and tell you that He loves you a *lot*? So much, in fact, that He gave up the most valuable thing He had—His Son— just so He could have the opportunity to build a close relationship with you. (John 3:16, anybody?)

The way God created you was not a mistake. Remember, He made the human race and He "saw that it was very good!" (Genesis 1:31). He calls you His "masterpiece" (Ephesians 2:10). He wants you to see yourself the way He sees you, but it may take some time. You may have to become more familiar with one particular fruit of the Spirit—patience. Your time of singleness is not wasted; it's preparation, and preparation requires patience.

Two of my favorite meals are Thanksgiving and Christmas dinners. Everything is baked with love, glazed with goodness, and cooked with care. The thing these meals have in common is the requirement of patience. The way I was raised, the planning, preparation, and execution of those meals can take up to a week. It's not quick drive-through food, nor is it convenient. If someone cooks these meals fast for you, I can guarantee it's not good and you should come to Thanksgiving or Christmas with my family instead. In the same way, when we desire relationships that are *mmm, mmm, good,* we may have to learn how to wait real good in our singleness.

Sync up with God's sequence: love God and build relationship with Him, love yourself and embrace your singleness, and then love others.

RESET

Today, in her late twenties, Diamond is a manager in the finance department of one of the largest corporations in Tulsa. I'm telling you, this is a lady who's got it going on. Her career is taking off, she has lots of friends, and she's helped out in so many ways at Transformation Church that I don't think any of the rest of us even realize.

But it wasn't always that way.

Diamond was sexually abused by a family member when she was a teenager. As a way to medicate the pain from that experience, she plunged into a wild lifestyle. For her first two years at the University of Oklahoma, she was partying and sleeping around more than she was attending her classes. But then she found Christ after being invited to a dorm Bible study, and her life started to change.

One of the things she decided to do differently was to stop dating entirely for a season. Instead of guys and partying, she would focus on healing the scars from her past, discovering herself, and working on her gifts. She asked a group of friends to hold her accountable for staying pure and learning to be a godly woman.

"I needed to reset my values," Diamond said to me. "My values about relationships were all set by culture and family members I'd observed, and the message it taught me was that I needed to be in a relationship at all times. I realized that wasn't true. I needed to discover myself before I was ready to be with a man."

Diamond says that her season of singleness prepared her for making life decisions. She transferred to the University of Tulsa to finish her bachelor's degree, then went right on to earn a master's at Michigan State before coming back to Tulsa to work. She turned down every date offer during those years. "Thanks, but I'm just not ready to date right now," she would say.

Recently Diamond has begun to date again, but it's much purer and more purposeful this time around. She knows the kind of man she needs to help her be the kind of woman she's becoming—a woman in Christ. She dates only if she thinks the guy will push her toward purpose.

"The only way to be sure what you're looking for," Diamond says, "is to find yourself."

"THE ONLY WAY TO BE SURE WHAT YOU'RE LOOKING FOR IS TO FIND YOURSELF."

I know exactly what Diamond means. To be whole for a relationship, she first needed to find herself in God.

SINGLE AND UNDER CONSTRUCTION

I know the world makes it seem like if you're single, you should stay ready to mingle, but—like Diamond found out—it's okay to be single and under construction. Singleness is a time for building a basis that will help your future relationships endure.

Therapists talk about the building blocks of a good marriage: communication, intimacy, honesty, and trust. All these are essential to a strong, healthy relationship, but building blocks must be stacked on a strong foundation. The only building materials God has to establish a marriage are you and your potential spouse. Even if you are dating or engaged, you are still technically single. Before you plan a big day with that beautiful white dress, the tux, the flowers, the photographer, and the church—before you even meet your spouse—you should prepare yourself.

God wants to help. He offers us the time necessary to develop the character, work ethic, intelligence, and emotional health that it will take to nurture a healthy relationship.

If I can echo the writer of Ecclesiastes, there is a time to be single and a time to date. Our time of singleness isn't meant to be a punishment or purgatory. It's God's way of providing us with a season of development and growth to prepare for the blessing to come. The more you come to understand this, the more you can take some of the pressure off yourself.

You aren't single because there's something wrong with you. Maybe you're single because God wants you to be. He's

SINGLE BUT NOT ALONE

When many people think of being single, they think of being alone, but those two things aren't the same. Being single is simply not having a romantic partner right now. The word *alone,* sounding like *loneliness,* suggests someone who lacks company and solidarity. It describes someone who has no friends, someone who feels left out.

You may be single, but "you are not alone." And I'm not saying that just because it's a good Michael Jackson lyric. It's the truth.

You are not alone. A lot of the single people I know have more active friendships than the people who are tied up in a serious dating relationship, engagement, or marriage. *You* have great friendship potential too.

Most importantly, even if no other person is with you at the moment, God is with you. He promises,

I will never fail you.
I will never abandon you. (HEBREWS 13:5)

madly in love with you; maybe He wants you all to Himself for a while. Being single doesn't make you insufficient or insignificant; it just means you have more time to develop and get to know yourself. I challenge you to use this time wisely. Singleness isn't an excuse to take a back seat on life but an opportunity to wholeheartedly pursue your own purpose.

God wants you to be self-aware in your singleness. This means recognizing your own faults and shortcomings so that you can allow Him to work on those areas and pray that your future spouse is doing the same, wherever that person is.

I am living proof that marriage pulls the sheet back on who you really are. I've been married for years, and my wife is still pointing out insecurities in my life that I didn't even know were there. "Oh, you're comparing yourself with others," she'll tell me. "Don't forget who you are."

I must admit, each time she does this, I tend to deny it. I insist that I'm not out of line . . . and then I realize she's right.

My wife exposes my shortcomings time and again. God has anointed her to reveal and uncover the things in my life that are not in line with Him and His plan, and I love her even more for that. We share accountability as partners and continuously call each other higher. We also married each other very young and have been together from the age of fourteen, so there is a *lot* to point out!

Natalie and I love each other so much, but we've had to endure some challenges that at times make us wish we'd spent the time before we were married allowing God to shape our character more. This is why the period of singleness is so important.

Now, there will still be times when our spouses speak truth to us, no matter how much we prepare before they come. We will never arrive at perfection, but we can help the process by entering into a relationship with a clear, honest sense of our true selves and how that truth will affect our future. If we use our singleness well, it can propel us further like maybe no other season in life can. When you are in relationship with God, even if you're not in relationship with a "special someone" here on earth, transformation is guaranteed and *all* your relationships will be blessed from it.

SO, YOU WANT TO BE MARRIED?

Marriage is such a strong covenant that God tries to convince us not to enter into it unless we are confident that we're ready. Many tend to view matrimony as a method of escape, but escaping your single life is not a reason to marry someone, even if he is tall and handsome with a killer smile. We must be careful not to be so drawn to the outward appearance that we neglect to recognize the inward condition.

Now, God knows the desires of your heart, and I'm certainly not trying to persuade you to give up on your dreams or in any way imply that you don't deserve or can't one day have a loving relationship with someone you're attracted to. (As a matter of fact, you *need* to be attracted to your spouse.) I'm just pointing out that maybe you've seen the advertised appeal of marriage and you've been drawn to it for the wrong reasons.

Many people tend to rush to get married because they think it will solve their loneliness problem. They get sick of being by themselves, so they long to join hands and hearts (and other things) with someone else. One big problem with that philosophy is that those they enter into relationship with might share the same issue. You're sick of yourself and think you plus somebody else will make it better—but what if that person is sick of herself too? We're almost trained to think this way: *Maybe this person can fix me.* By the time we realize our mistake, it's already too late, because when broken people hook up, they end up becoming more broken together. Nobody is perfect, but we should all be progressing.

The partners we choose often have their own problems and equally unrealistic expectations. They can't fix us any more

MARRIAGE IS NOT A HIDEOUT FROM SINGLENESS BUT A HAVEN FOR BUILDING WHOLENESS.

than we can fix them. Only God can. Marriage was never intended to be a hideout from singleness but rather a haven for building wholeness.

Sadly, most people who enter into marriage don't really know what it takes, and that's probably a major reason why about 45 percent of marriages in America end in divorce! What if your flight attendant announced, just before takeoff, that your Boeing 737 jet had little more than one out of two chances of safely arriving at your planned destination? Most of us would be taking the bus.

Most people nowadays enter into marriage haphazardly, neglecting the process that will help prepare them to succeed in it. That process works best while you are single, when you don't have to actively consider someone else's feelings, emotions, wants, desires, and needs. In many cases, people end up getting married but continue trying to explore and figure out their singleness to the extent that they neglect their commitment to the relationship; they end up trying to be unified in marriage and exclusively single at the same time because they never really took the time to embrace being single. That's how issues like infidelity can creep into a marriage relationship.

If you're married and the marriage is in trouble, look back at your singleness for the source of your problem. Perhaps you didn't learn basic character-shaping qualities, like patience, self-control, and grace, while you were single.

Or maybe you didn't realize how much habits like proper hygiene could affect another person. Hygiene might not sound that serious, but it's the dishes-in-the-sink issues like this that cause repeated friction. I learned this lesson the hard way in the early years of our marriage. Let's just say one time when I tried to get close with my boo, she said, "Boy, you smell like booty!" and exiled me to the shower.

Maybe you're like me and you've struggled with insecurities that have led you to do things you wouldn't normally do just to win another person's attention or affection. You need to learn some things about yourself before you collide your world with someone else's. It's important to consider how you process information, resolve conflict, and receive love and how you perceive the world around you while it's just you and God. Spending time looking in the mirror at yourself will save you so much time later on when another person is in the picture with you.

Sure, you can evolve and change while you're in a relationship. As a matter of fact, you should. But it's best to be honest about where you are in the process before you add the complication/companionship of another person and all his issues into the equation.

That's what my friend Chuck taught me. He's on his second marriage. Once, I asked him what went wrong in his first marriage.

For a guy who is normally smiling and joking, Chuck got an unusually serious look on his face. "I wasn't ready for marriage back then," he said. "I didn't spend enough time knowing myself to be able to communicate my needs to her."

"But your current marriage is going better, right?" I asked.

"Yeah, but only because I had a period between my marriages to figure out what my issues were."

When you get into marriage, you become responsible for conditions and sacrifices that you don't have as a single person. Before you take on these extra responsibilities, I suggest that you learn to take care of yourself. Get to know you. If you don't take the time to get to know yourself while you're single, you can pick what (or whom) you think you want, but that thing or person won't end up satisfying your true needs.

What would happen if you intentionally took the time to work on yourself before you entered into a relationship with someone else? Even if you never have a long-term relationship or get married, knowing yourself better is going to make your life richer and more productive.

IT'S "I" TIME

When I was in the ninth grade, I quit playing basketball to focus on music. I was a good ball player, and my coaches tried to convince me to come back, but I recognized that I wasn't going to the NBA. I chose to prioritize what mattered to me, what I considered my purpose. For me, that was music. I poured four and a half years into pursuing my music goals. During that time, I had friends. I had relationships. I was far from lonely, yet I was single in that I didn't shut my life down to be in relationships. I maintained my purpose and my drive for music.

God wants the same level of commitment from you during your season of singleness. You can spend your time pursuing all sorts of opportunities and develop relationships as long as you don't neglect to spend time pursuing Him.

Singleness is the time for "I": invest, imagine, and inspire. *Invest* in what you want to see grow in your life. *Imagine*

INVEST, IMAGINE, AND INSPIRE. what you could be tomorrow if you started today. And *inspire* others by using everything you have now to make a difference.

Let me give you a few practical examples. You could invest in your nonromantic friendships, which could then flourish into lifelong community. Or you could invest in your creative passion, which could turn into a career one day. You could imagine yourself financially free and start learning to manage your money better. Or imagine where in the world you'd want to travel and plan the trip. One of the most impactful things you can do is take time to inspire others by sharing your story or mentoring someone else.

When you use your season of singleness to understand and improve yourself while getting closer to the God who made you, it's like taking a leap of faith—it's a sign that you trust in the outcome of God's plan for your life.

SINGLE TO THE MAX

Remember that in the beginning God did not make Adam and Eve's marriage. He made a single man first. It was only after Adam was working in the garden and enjoying contentment and fulfillment in God that He introduced marriage and relationship.

Now, the Bible doesn't say how long Adam was single before God gave him Eve. I think this was on purpose, because if God had given us a timetable for our singleness, we'd all be more concerned with the countdown than the process. Everyone's season of singleness may not be the same amount of time, but it has the same importance.

Wear the s-word proudly. Maximize your singleness. Make the most of it.

And then keep working on you for the rest of your life.

4 INTENTIONAL DATING

The soul needs beauty for a soul mate
When the soul wants, the soul waits

—U2, "A Man and a Woman"

Like I said earlier, I was fifteen and Natalie was fourteen when we started dating. We got married nine years later. I'd like to say our dating relationship was smooth for that whole nine-year period, but that would be a lie . . . especially for the time I call our ten months of insanity.

When we were young adults, Natalie wanted to get more serious about our relationship. She started talking about marriage.

I wasn't ready for that. I guess I got scared or selfish or something. 'Cause that's when I started thinking, *I've been with Nat for several years now. Maybe I need to see what else is out there. How can I settle down with a girl when she's the only one I've ever been with?*

That wasn't the Spirit of God inside me talking. That was culture talking. That was all the rap videos, the locker-room talk, and the voices of people telling me I was too young to settle down. That's what the Enemy wanted me to believe. It was like the serpent suggesting to Adam and Eve that they should eat the forbidden fruit because God was holding something back from them, even though He was really just protecting them from harm.

At the time, I was filling in on drums for a girl group. One of the girls in the band let me know she liked me. I was interested in her too. So, I told Natalie, "I want to take a break from seeing you and spend some time with God." That sounded righteous, but it was actually so ratchet.

Natalie soon found out what was going on. It broke her heart.

I moved on from the band girl to another girl. I started sneaking in this girl's window in the middle of the night, sending texts I would never have wanted anybody else to see, watching porn when I couldn't be with her. Meanwhile, in retaliation, Natalie started seeing another guy. It got crazy on both sides as we forgot who we were and abandoned our plans and our principles. We both became sexually active with other people and so we couldn't give our virginity to each other when we got married.

Finally, we both came to our senses and God brought us back together. But the consequences continued—ten months of insanity led to ten years of insecurity. Because of what had happened, neither of us was quite sure we could trust the other one. Even after years of marriage, Natalie would be watching whom I was hugging at church. And I would remind her of what she'd done wrong. Actually, both of us were faithful to each other, but we still had these suspicions. It was horrible.

God has finally healed us of all that doubt and mistrust. But I don't want to forget what I learned: I almost lost the best thing I ever had in my life because I lost my focus. I lost my aim. There's nobody better than Natalie for helping me become the man God wants me to be, and like an idiot, I put my goals and purposes in jeopardy.

With all the motivation that comes from my own mistakes and from the mistakes of so many other people I've talked to, I'm now going to move on from the topic of the previous chapter—the special opportunities that singleness can provide—to talk about the dating phase in the relationship sequence.

Maybe you're thinking, *Man, I'm past that stage. I'm married.*

Well, hang on, because this chapter is still for you. I'll give you three reasons why. First, some of the principles in this chapter apply to how you choose all kinds of long-term friends and partners in your life. You can easily see the crossover. Second, even if you're not dating, I'm sure you've got friends, children, grandchildren, or others in your life who *are* at that stage of life. Don't you wish you'd had more godly input back when you were dating? Well, now you can be that kind of adviser to others who are dating—*if* you have the right advice to give. And third, the decisions you made when you were dating are still impacting your marriage now, especially if you've not dealt with them in the right way.

Hosea 4:6 says, "My people are destroyed for lack of knowledge" (NKJV). If we think we can just figure out dating on our own, that means we're simply following the bad examples in the world around us. Trust me, other people's #RelationshipGoals don't look as good in real life as they do on Instagram. So, use knowledge of godly living to avoid destructive experiences like the ones I had during my ten months of insanity or to help others avoid them. And if you are dating and have made mistakes (I sure did!), it's not too late now to learn what dating is for and how to go about it.

Whatever your relationship goals are, you're not going to reach them by doing the kind of dating most single people do—*recreational dating*. Instead, you gotta try what I call *in-*

tentional dating. Recreational dating is dating that's focused on having fun and getting experiences. Recreational dating is the opposite of aiming at a goal; it's like shooting at everything. Intentional dating, though, is being purposeful. It's fun, too, but it preserves purity. Most importantly, it's driven by a clear goal: to determine whether the person you are dating is right for you to marry. It's all about moving toward the covenant of marriage, with the right person, in the right way, in the right time.

> **INTENTIONAL DATING IS ALL ABOUT MOVING TOWARD THE COVENANT OF MARRIAGE.**

Come along with me as we zoom in to take a closer look at both kinds of dating and where they lead.

AIMLESSNESS IN DATING

Recreational dating is like, *I'll date him, then I'll date him, then I'll date him* (or *her, her, her*). It's one-night stands, impulsive infatuations, short-term relationships, and overlapping love affairs, usually with plenty of drama and complications. It's focused pretty much all on the present, with little thought about the future. Because you don't take it seriously regarding commitment and covenant, it's very easy to get casual about the physical.

That stuff sticks with you forever. You can be in a crowded room and somebody introduces you to another person: "Oh, I know him; we used to date." Possibly meaning you hooked up. Or "She's a friend." A friend with benefits, that might be.

Even if the person you're with is somebody you've been

seeing for a while now, if somebody asked you, "What do you see in your future?" you'd just have a vague, blurry image. "Yeah, one day we might get married, I think, maybe."

This kind of dating isn't harmless. It can be devastating. Just think about it: How many relationships have you, or people you know, gotten into where you have invested time and effort into something that would only take from you? Your heart gets hardened. Your self-esteem shrinks. You find yourself moving further and further from God.

And there's more: open your heart to the wrong person and you let him discourage your dream. You used to be passionate about something. But you got

OPEN YOUR HEART TO THE WRONG PERSON AND YOU LET HIM DISCOURAGE YOUR DREAM.

with the wrong person, and it started to crush what God placed inside you. The relationship is over, but you're left in a place where you don't believe in yourself anymore. You lost time, you lost vision, and you lost hope because you were in a wrongly aligned relationship.

First Corinthians 15:33 says, "Bad company corrupts good character." That applies across the board in our influential relationships. Its wisdom is clearest, though, when you see good girls get with bad dudes, or good dudes get with bad girls, and just like that, they turn into different people. They're doing stuff they didn't used to do. Stuff that isn't what God wants and doesn't help them fulfill their purpose.

Let's just say it straight out—recreational dating doesn't work. Even a committed long-term relationship, as the saying goes, often leaves people feeling like they lost out. Over and over again, I've seen it with dating couples: they sleep together, they eat together, they have a cell-phone plan together—basically it's a fake marriage with everything but the covenant. But all that makes the relationship harder to get out of than it was to get into. The breakup, when it finally comes, is traumatic. Instead of finding a lifetime mate, they've lost so much.

I call this the dating deficit. The modern way of dating—recreational dating with a vague hope that maybe one relationship will finally go somewhere—doesn't deliver what it promises.

If the dating deficit sounds painfully familiar, then let me say straight at you: God loves you too much and He put too much purpose in you for you to be wasting your relational life with no aim. You've got to start rethinking how you do relationships. As 1 Corinthians 15:34 says, "Think carefully about what is right."

And then it says, "Stop sinning." Just stop. Please, I'm begging you: stop. Why? Because if you're making decisions in a sinful state, your flesh will always lie to you. So, let that door close. Repent. Turn. And begin again.

The sooner, the better, especially if you've been stuck in a dead-end relationship for a long time.

DATING IS NOT A DESTINATION

It surprises me how many people date for long periods of time. Like, *This is where we at. We ain't going nowhere else. We're satisfied.*

"How long y'all been dating?"

"Fifteen years."

"What did you just say to me?! There is a kid in high school who is as old as you've been dating? What are you talking about?"

And so, if you've been dating a while, the thing you have to start asking yourself is, Why? *Why haven't we taken that step into covenant? Why haven't we moved past where we've been into commitment?* Is it because you don't trust the other person? Because you don't know any better? Because the institution of marriage has somehow left a bad taste in your mouth? Or what?

Your reason, whatever it is, does not outweigh God's plan for the covenant (sacred, lasting agreement) of marriage. So, if you've been dating long enough to know each other and feel like you're right for each other long term, then move beyond dating. You are delaying what God would have for you.

I was in an airport the other day with my friend Charles. We got off one plane and had to catch a connecting plane. To get to the other gate, we rode the tram from terminal A to terminal C. That took us to our intended target, our new place.

That's when I realized something: dating is transportation to a relational target. This dating thing is not supposed to be the place where we stay. It's supposed to be the place that takes us to marriage. It's supposed to take us to covenant.

DATING IS TRANSPORTATION TO A RELATIONAL TARGET.

At the airport, they don't want you to stay on the tram. I know that because they don't put a lot of seats in there. They want you to hang on just long enough so you can get to the destination.

When you date too long, you are putting yourself in a position to sit down in a place that was supposed to just be transportation. When you do that, it will be uncomfortable because you were never meant to stay there. God wants you to arrive at the intended destination or get off.

Charles and I were at terminal A, going to terminal C, but between those is terminal B. Maybe you need to get off at terminal B in your dating relationship. Just say, "This is not for me. I don't need to be here anymore. I don't need to be surrounded in this company. I'll get off and I'll walk."

I know that means you're back to looking for somebody else to date. That's okay. Really. In fact, taking the long route sometimes builds stamina in you that will produce what you really need. You may not find the one you're supposed to be with while riding the dating train with the same person endlessly. In fact, it may just be that when you get off the thing and start walking, you finally find your true destination.

In the next chapter, we'll be getting to know when to put an end to a dating relationship. For now, all I'm trying to say to you is, dating is not supposed to be a destination. It's supposed to be transportation to where you really want to go.

DATING FOR THE GLORY OF GOD

I've told you what dating isn't. It isn't just playtime. It isn't pretending like you're married. It isn't treating a season like it's a lifetime. That's messed up, all of it.

So, how *should* we be dating?

Now, the truth is, the Bible doesn't say much about dating or courting. But it is very clear on what type of company we should keep, the boundaries we should set in relationships, and the character of the people we should choose as our life partners. All this gives us more than enough clues to guide us in dating. Let me give you the big, broad picture of how I look at this.

First Corinthians 10:31 says, "Whether you eat or drink, or whatever you do, do it all for the glory of God." *Whatever you do* includes dating. When you date, you should do it for the glory of God. Talk about a concept that is totally different from what our culture promotes! Talk about a relationship goal! Dating for the glory of God.

How do you do that?

You date in an intentional and holy way. Or you might call it dating with purpose. It's dating with the end in mind, wanting to do what pleases the Lord.

To state what I hope is obvious, I'm not trying to stop you from dating. And I don't want to turn dating into work. I'm just trying to get you to do dating differently than most people do it. You might date *a lot*. That's cool. But be selective about whom you're dating, and while you're having fun, also be evaluating what's going on so that you can either bring a misguided relationship to an end before it gets too costly or move it toward a goal if it seems right.

DON'T BE IN A HURRY TO COMMIT YOUR MIND, HEART, OR BODY TO ANOTHER PERSON.

This is dating where you're in no hurry to commit your mind, heart, or body to the other person. You've got some boundaries in place. And boundaries are biblical. Boundaries are one of the things that God uses to help us reach purpose. It preserves who He's made us to be at our core:

Guard your heart above all else,

    for it determines the course of your life.

      (Proverbs 4:23)

Having boundaries is a way of saying, "I'm gonna set my eyes and my heart on the things that please God. I got gates. You can't get in that easy."

Do you not see how important it is to put up the fence? String the barbed wire around your heart? Get the guard dogs out there? Because if you don't, you will allow wrong things to influence your heart. And why does the condition of your heart matter? Because "it determines the course of your life."

In case you're in a dating relationship right now, let me help you ask yourself the two most basic questions to determine whether you are dating to the glory of God.

1. Is the Person I'm Dating Bringing Glory to God?

A dating relationship isn't going to bring glory to God unless both people are following God. So, regardless of what the other person says about her faith, does how she lives, how she talks, what she watches and listens to prove she really loves God?

I've heard women say something like this: "My man, he's smart and got a good job. Yeah, he's got some issues. But I look past all of that because he is a good person at his core and God is showing me He wants me to be somebody who helps him grow."

What do I say to that? "Naw! The man is supposed to lead *you*!"

I might ask a bro what attracted him to the woman he's dating. If he's honest, he might say to me, "She wears the leggings. She looks *good* in the leggings. I *like* that she wears the leggings."

My reaction? "If she likes showing off her shape for men, do you think that just because she's started dating you, she's stopped showing off for other men? They like the leggings too."

I'm not saying that anyone has to be perfect, but he has to be progressing to become the next version of who God is calling him to be. I'm being this specific to let you know that until you understand that the person you're seeing should be living his life to glorify God, you're starting off with some wrong ingredients.

2. Is How We're Dating Bringing Glory to God?

Are you two in the back of a car in a parking lot somewhere steaming up the windows? If somebody were watching you two together, would your witness be destroyed? Would you be able to say anything about your relationship with Jesus if people saw your text messages? (Drops mic.)

I'm just trying to give you a formula to see whether this relationship is good for you or not.

This whole topic of sex is so big that I'm going to devote two chapters to it. But you can be overly intimate without even going to sex and still bring dishonor to God.

Depending on the who and the how, if you want a God-glorifying dating relationship, you might need to break off a relationship even if the person you're dating is supposedly a Christian like you. But I've got to address another situation that is even more basic than that. I've seen so many brothers and sisters foolishly get themselves into trouble when it never had to be an issue at all.

DON'T EVEN GO THERE

Genesis says that God made Eve "just right" for Adam (2:18). And Adam was just right for Eve. They were a team that belonged together.

Intentional dating is looking for that kind of partnership—the partnership that is "just right."

Recreational dating too often sticks you with the opposite kind—the kind that is "just right now."

"Unequally yoked" is a big biblical term for "Don't get with the wrong person just 'cause they fine and they got a few dimes." That's not worth it, because you will have a life of misery trying to go one way when he's going the other way. I mean, you'll literally begin to feel the distance. If one is moving and the other one is not, you're gonna begin to sense that tension.

Now, I know that may sound harsh, but think about it. Being *yoked* was a term used for oxen back in the day. The wooden beam that went over the oxen's necks was called a yoke. You would never put a strong ox next to a weak ox because the two wouldn't be able to achieve the goal of pulling a plow in a straight line without bringing strain on one and potentially damaging the other. So farmers tried to get two oxen that were compatible: "equally yoked." Being equally yoked allowed the oxen to achieve the goal.

Can you see how this applies to relationships? Insisting on being equally yoked doesn't mean you're a religious bigot. It is for the good of two single people who are attracted to each other and even more so for a married couple. It's about peace and well-being in the present and productivity in the future.

The "unequally yoked" scripture in the Message version says, "Don't become partners with those who reject God.

How can you make a partnership out of right and wrong? That's not partnership; that's war" (2 Corinthians 6:14). *War.* Isn't that how a lot of relationships look? If you're saying "We're always just fighting," you might be with somebody who's not going the same direction as you.

The scripture goes on: "Is light best friends with dark? Does Christ go strolling with the Devil? Do trust and mistrust hold hands?" (verses 14–15). The answer to all those questions is no. Jesus was the friend of sinners, and so should we be. But that's different than partnering—yoking up in a romantic relationship, a business partnership, or whatever—with those who have totally different loyalties in their faith than we do.

It's bad enough in a dating relationship to be unequally yoked; it's worse in marriage. So, if you're single, don't even get started on that road. Somebody wants to date you who doesn't care about God like you do? Then remember that sometimes being intentional in dating means not even starting up together. Or you're already dating somebody and the way she's acting and what she's trying to get you to do are making it clear her faith isn't what she said it was? It's time to slip out of that yoke and move on.

IF HE'S NOT MATEABLE, HE'S NOT DATEABLE.

Follow this simple rule to save yourself heartache, conflict, and a bigger risk than you think of getting pulled away from Christ: *If he's not mateable, he's not dateable.* That simply means, if you wouldn't marry the person, don't go out with him.

Find someone who's going the same direction as you: not perfect but making progress in following Jesus.

INTENTIONAL FRIENDSHIP

"We met here at Transformation. We like each other. We want to spend time together and see where it goes," Brandon said. His new girlfriend, Taylor, nodded along. "But we know we can't do dating like we did with other people in the past."

"Why is that?" I asked.

"Well . . . ," Taylor said.

It turns out, in the past Taylor had had a series of sexual relationships with men, most of them short-term relationships but a couple of them more long-term, shacking-up situations. One of her boyfriends, a thug, had involved her in criminal activity, and she was still trying to negotiate her way out of jail time.

Meanwhile, Brandon had been involved in a number of sexual relationships with people of both sexes. Most recently he'd been living with a man. He had issues with masculinity and any type of authority.

In other words, Brandon and Taylor had had relatively normal relationships by the world's standards. And they'd had the normal results too—a lot of pain and confusion. Every relationship seemed like it took more than it gave. But both had found Christ in the past year and had been radically transformed by God, and now they were ready to do their relationship differently.

"Let's get together with Natalie," I said. "We have a different approach we want to share with you."

Nat and I started meeting occasionally with Taylor and Brandon. We started them on a program we have that sort of formalizes the intentional dating process for people who want that. I call it intentional friendship. After all, friendship is the

IF YOU'VE MESSED UP

Maybe you've started a new relationship with the best intentions . . . but fell morally yet again, just like in the old days.

My advice? When that happens, reset real quick. Don't fall and stay there. Go to God, be honest and tell Him you're sorry, and get back to pleasing Him right away. That's what repenting is.

God won't beat you up over your mistake. If He knows your heart is in the right place, He wants to move you ahead even more than you want to.

The godly may trip seven times, but they will get up again. (PROVERBS 24:16)

If we confess our sins to him, he is faithful and just to forgive us our sins and to cleanse us from all wickedness. (1 JOHN 1:9)

cornerstone of every relationship, and a good friendship is formed over time.

During this time, we had Taylor and Brandon talk about their fears and expectations. We had them agree with each other on some boundaries for their physical relationship. And we had them discuss topics around relationship with each other. Then we got back together to debrief.

I asked them what the intentional friendship time had meant to them.

Brandon said, "It focused our passions. It helped each of us clarify what we want to do in life and think about how we might be able to help each other. We like each other more than ever, and we want to keep spending time together."

Not every couple who goes through our intentional friendship program stays together, but Taylor and Brandon soon realized they wanted each other. A year after I met them, I had the honor of performing their wedding. The ceremony was a celebration of love and a testimony of God's ability to turn people around when they submit themselves to Him.

NINETY DAYS TO ERASING THE DATING DEFICIT

There's a widespread dating deficit in our day because recreational dating doesn't deliver what it promises. And you know what they say about the definition of *insanity*—it's doing the same thing over and over again and expecting different results. How about trying a different approach to dating?

I'm going to teach you the same process Natalie and I taught to Brandon and Taylor as well as to other couples who have been burned by relationships in the past and want to try an approach that leads to finding their mates without trashing their

> RECREATIONAL DATING DOESN'T DELIVER WHAT IT PROMISES.

hearts in the process. In a time when relationships become "Facebook official" overnight, you need to take time—without everybody else applying pressure or giving an opinion—to see if you're really attracted to the other person, if your values line up, and if you can help each other become who you're meant to be.

Wouldn't you like a clear path to a healthy relationship?

Take ninety days to get to know each other without pressure. *Gasp!* "Ninety days?!" Hey, it's just three months, less than the length of a football season. That's not such a long time to spend forming an intentional friendship, which might lead to intentional dating, which might lead to marriage, now is it?

If you can, go through this process with advisers in the form of a trusted married couple who are wise in the ways of the Lord. The first time you meet with them, it's like an on-ramp to a relationship. The last time you meet with them, at the end of ninety days, it's like an off-ramp to get out of the relationship easily if it hasn't worked out. Or else it's like a green light to continue the journey and see where it goes.

1. Discuss Your Relationship Fears

Write down your three greatest fears of being in relationship, and share them with each other. Maybe they include "getting pressured to be more physical than I want." Or "telling my deep secrets and having you share them with your friends." Or "not being treated like I'm important." Or "having my hopes built up, only to have them ruined."

By doing this, you each know something about your expectations. You get a chance to be protective of each other's hearts. And this vulnerability provides accountability later on. For example, if she said she wants to still be a virgin when she marries and he is pushing to have sex, that shows he doesn't care about her values.

2. Agree on Boundaries

No matter how old or how experienced you are, if you want to have a pure relationship and not create too strong of a physical tie before marriage, then you need to agree from the outset about what you will or will not do. You may be thinking, *I don't need boundaries. I'm grown.* Well, so are your pain, disappointments, and frustrations. Boundaries aren't bad; they're actually a blessing.

These are a few rules for the road so you don't get in an accident on the journey.

- *Set a curfew.* Every date needs an ending time. Decide that one of you is always going to go home at midnight or whatever other time you agree on.
- *What's a no go for touch?* Maybe it's hugs that last longer than thirty seconds. Or French kissing. Or whatever. Know the triggers that could take you all the way to sex.
- *What else would help?* Maybe you'll agree not to watch movies with sex scenes in them. Or not to send each other notes or texts that are too suggestive. A lot of couples agree to never chill in a horizontal position (lying down on a couch or bed), only in a vertical position.

These kinds of boundaries may seem petty, and they're not meant to be legalistic, but they have a way of helping people keep from succumbing to natural temptations. They create a safe place for you to learn about each other. They encourage less touching and more talking.

3. Have Focused Conversations

It can be hard to make conversation when you don't know each other well. So, read a book about relationship and discuss it. It will help you get to know each other and start sensing if you're right for each other.

For example, I encourage couples to read Gary Chapman's *The Five Love Languages*. It will give you a peek into how the other person works and help you frame the relationship. For example, if one person loves gifts, the other one had better be prepared to open his wallet from time to time. It can also help you avoid mistakes. If somebody loves quality time and the other one loves physical touch, you'd better set strong physical boundaries because one is going to want to sit on the couch all the time and the other one is going to want to be touched—and that's a recipe for a baby.

After ninety days, have a conversation to see where you stand. Are you attracted to each other? Green light or red flag?

I always encourage people to pay attention to *patterns,* not *potential.* All of us have the potential to do better in our weak areas, but can we live with each other's patterns? For instance, she may seem flirtatious to you, but she says it's just her personality—she's bubbly and likes talking to everybody. Can you live with that? Transformation in this area may come eventually, but even if so, there's no timetable on it.

You may want to go ahead with more dating together, hopefully leading to engagement and marriage, or you may decide to call it quits. (The next chapter will help you more in making this decision.) If you do decide to end it here, hopefully the breakup will happen without all the painful ripping apart that can happen when a dating couple is too tightly bonded. Instead of feeling like you lost, you can feel like you gained—you had some fun, you got to know somebody else, and you picked up some relationship tools that you can use next time around.

Your relationship goal of marriage is still alive and healthy.

SHINE

Let's be real. Dating for just fun and sex and going from one person to the next can be pretty exciting. At least for a while, until the pain and numbness set in. So, even though you might *want* to want to do holy and intentional dating, you might not be sure you really *want* to do it . . . if you follow what I mean. Or even if you really *want* to do it, you may not be sure you *can* do it, because it will be so easy to slip back into your old ways.

Again, this is true in nonromantic relationships too. Will you really spend time doing the due diligence on the integrity of the people in your business's supply chain? Will you be able to resist when your old homeboy, the one who is still using the substances you've given up, gets back in touch and wants to hang with you? You might not be so sure you can do the right thing.

Nat and I went through our own ten months of insanity. Others have experienced the insanity of the modern way of doing relationships. We need a different way of dating. And we need to believe that *we really can make a change.*

Look at this anchor scripture for *Relationship Goals:* "God is working in you, giving you the desire and the power to do what pleases him" (Philippians 2:13). When it comes to your dating relationships or any relationships, when you invite God into the situation, He'll give you the *desire* to do it right and then He'll fund it— He'll give you the *power* to do it in a

> WHEN IT COMES TO YOUR RELATIONSHIPS, GOD WILL GIVE YOU THE *DESIRE* AND THE *POWER* TO DO IT RIGHT.

way that pleases Him. That's how good our God is. Can I get an amen?

That same passage goes on to say, "Live clean, innocent lives as children of God, shining like bright lights in a world full of crooked and perverse people" (verse 15). Your dating relationships should be able to shine. And that will make it easier for the whole rest of your relational life to shine too.

5 DOES IT NEED TO END?

Keep talking that mess, that's fine
But could you walk and talk at the same time?
—BEYONCÉ, "Irreplaceable"

Is it destiny, or is it fate
Or have I found my soulmate?
—DRE, "Soulmate"

Quick recap from the last chapter: Dating is supposed to be just a relational phase. You're not supposed to go on and on with it as long as you're into the other person and having fun together or just because you get comfortable. In intentional dating, you're trying to find out if the person you're dating is right for you as marriage material. Sooo . . .

Eventually this phase needs to come to an end one way or the other. I mean, put a ring on it—or call it quits.

Can we be honest? How many of us have wasted time in relationships before? The answer is practically all of us. We've spent a lot of unnecessary time in relationships that will not benefit us in the end.

> PUT A RING ON IT OR CALL IT QUITS.

If a card came when we started each relationship and told us how it was going to end, we would stop a lot of relationships much sooner. What if a card said, "You're going to waste four years with this person. You're going to have lower self-esteem, and you're going to hate everybody around you when it ends. Do you still want this relationship?" You would be like, "Heck, no. That's not what I want." But many times it's hard to see the whole picture when we're in it.

And as usual, what I'm going to say in this chapter doesn't apply just to dating relationships. It applies to all kinds of influential relationships in our lives. It may be hard for you to see that you've been in business with the wrong business partner when you're already working together. It may be hard for you to figure out that a friend is not good for you after you've been going everywhere together and you've celebrated life achievements together. But these kinds of relationships, just like dating relationships, might reach a point where we need to end them.

Whatever relationships you're in, I want to help you see whether you can better answer the question, Does it need to end?

• • •

Let me give you a caveat here. If you are married, some of the things I talk about in this chapter might reveal issues or problems in your marriage. Believe it or not, that's an awesome thing for you because it shows you what you can work on with your spouse. But let me be clear: I'm *not* asking you to consider ending the marriage.

Malachi says that marriage is sacred and that God hates divorce (2:13–16). A covenant has been established between you and your spouse. There are some reasons divorce needs to happen, and I'll be getting to that in chapter 8, but if you're married, recognizing the problems I mention in this chapter shouldn't send you to a divorce lawyer. It should send you to counseling.

That doesn't mean this chapter is irrelevant to you. Like I said, you're going to be able to apply it to other relationships in your life. But your marriage relationship? God wants you to fight for that one! There's a beautiful story that comes when God brings back to life a marriage that seemed like it was dying.

. . .

So now, let's get to the main point. If you've been with somebody awhile, you might have found out a lot of things about him (or yourself) that lead you to decide you've got to have that tough breaking-up conversation. But one thing you should never, ever overlook is if you're with somebody who's getting in the way of the plans and purposes you think God is calling you to.

Nobody's perfect. You ain't perfect. Your pookie ain't perfect. Absolutely. This isn't even about rejecting somebody because she's not hot enough or she's got an annoying habit or—God forbid—she doesn't match up with some retouched Instagram #RelationshipGoals photo you've got in the back of your mind. It's about figuring out if there's an issue in the relationship so serious it's keeping you from who you're supposed to be in Christ.

I don't know the details of your relationship, so I can't tell you if you need to break it off or not. Only *you* can decide that, while you're trying your best to hear God's will for you. All I'm saying is, if the shoe fits . . . I mean, if you are size 10.5, and these kicks I'm giving you are maybe a 10, then try them on and see if they might be worth buying.

MATCH MADE IN HEAVEN?

I have two close friends, T and Valeria. After being in the same circles for years, they decided they liked each other and wanted to date. They both had dedicated relationships with God, were walking in purpose, and had God-given influence with others before they started dating.

It seemed like a match made in heaven . . . but it turned out to be more like a professional wrestling match. Harsh words, controlling behaviors, irrational attitudes, and emotional turmoil were the chokeholds of this relationship. It was just a matter of time before one was pinned down, with the referee counting "1, 2, 3 . . ." and the match (you know, their dating relationship) was over.

Like many people, I was kind of surprised when these two great people had such an awful relationship. When Valeria and T talked to me separately about the reasons for their breakup, they both said that their relationship together took priority over their relationship with God. And then I understood. Dating > God is always a dangerous equation because we're left with our feelings as our guide as opposed to getting direction and wisdom from God.

Earlier I posed the question, Does it need to end? It's not idle speculation. In the case of Valeria and T, it *had* to end because it started affecting the things they knew they were purposed to do. And for many other dating couples, their happiness today and their blessing in the future hang on the decision they will make.

QUITTERS DO WIN

Think about this:

- When God wants to bless you, how does He do it? He sends people into your life.
- When the devil wants to distract you or destroy you, how does he do it? He sends people into your life.

If people who come into our lives are either a blessing or a curse, it's up to us to decipher, Is this relationship going to push me toward what God has for me, or is it keeping me from what God has for me?

Another way to put it: some relationships in your life may be more liabilities than assets. (For the nonaccountants, liabilities take from you; assets give to you.) So, what relationships in your life are taking from you? Taking peace? Taking joy? Taking time? Taking something you can never get back? You might have people in your life who are always negative, people who are always creating drama, people who tell you the truth but it always has a bend toward what's wrong in life. They're sucking and they're taking and they're making it harder for you to be who you were made to be.

SOME RELATIONSHIPS MAY BE MORE LIABILITIES THAN ASSETS.

It's God's plan that the relationships in our lives are supposed to be helping us and moving us toward fulfillment. The whole reason I wrote this book is so that I could help others win in relationship. You can't win in relationship if the person close to you is blocking your progress.

So, take an inventory. Write down a list of your acquaintances, friends, bros, sisters, business colleagues, mentors, students, relatives, associates, teammates, clients, followers, fans, supporters, boyfriend/girlfriend, baby mama/baby daddy, friend with benefits, just friend, fiancé/fiancée, spouse, spiritual leader, pastor—whomever you want. My question is, Are they adding value to you, or are they taking real value from you?

I've asked God to help me answer that question for my own relationships.

He said, "Michael, some of the problems you face are a result of the people you embrace." I knew what He meant. There were people in my life who were greedy, who didn't care about me or care about what God cares about. So, I made the intentional decision to invest only in relationships that are reciprocal. In other words, others bring something to the table as well. It has deepened and enriched my relationships and saved me so much time and heartache, as the people I'm embracing embrace me back. Have you ever tried to give a hug to someone who doesn't want to hug you back? It's awkward and it honestly sucks.

Let me tell you something else I've learned. When you start evaluating and looking at your life history, you might realize that you tend to attract the same kind of negative people over and over. Like, maybe you're a woman who has had serial problems with "bad boys." You know the type of guy I'm talking about—edgy, a rebel, the guy you would never bring home to your mom. You get rid of one and he just comes back with a different face. You think, *Forget you, Gerald. I ain't never going out with a bad boy again.* Then Ricky comes along, and he's a bad boy too. Then you get rid of Ricky, and now you're with Ramon, another one of the same kind. You get rid of Ramon. Then it's Lawrence.

TRUST IS REWARDED

What you place your faith in is more important than how much faith you have. So, if losing the security or familiarity of a relationship (even though you know it hasn't been good for you) makes you nervous, trust God to lead you through the time of breakup and take care of you on the other side. He's faithful.

Check out these verses that have comforted believers for thousands of years:

Trust in the LORD with all your heart;
    do not depend on your own understanding.
Seek his will in all you do,
    and he will show you which path to take.
        (PROVERBS 3:5-6)

You will keep in perfect peace
    all who trust in you,
    all whose thoughts are fixed on you! (ISAIAH 26:3)

Don't be afraid, for I am with you.
    Don't be discouraged, for I am your God.
I will strengthen you and help you.
    I will hold you up with my victorious right hand.
        (ISAIAH 41:10)

Don't let your hearts be troubled. Trust in God, and trust also in me. (JOHN 14:1)

The Father who knows all hearts knows what the Spirit is saying, for the Spirit pleads for us believers in harmony with God's own will. And we know that God causes everything to work together for the good of those who love God and are called according to his purpose for them. (ROMANS 8:27-28)

The common denominator in a situation like this is . . . you. Learn something from it. The problems you keep facing are because of the kind of person you are repeatedly embracing. You need to get rid of all of that type of people from your life and find some other kind of guy. Scripture says you should.

Look at Hebrews 12:1: "Let us strip off every weight that slows us down." The verse specifically mentions one kind of weight—"the sin that so easily trips us up." But there are other kinds of weights and burdens, including relational liabilities.

Every relationship that is not moving you toward purpose is weighing you down. Like, maybe you're dating somebody who's insecure and you're always wasting time trying to explain yourself because your boo thinks you have an ulterior motive. When you try to say something constructive to help her, she thinks you're coming at her because you're jealous of her. But that's not it at all. Is all this helping either one of you, really?

Who is around you that's slowing you down?

In Hebrews, this whole idea is set in the scene of a footrace in a big stadium, with a finish line at the end of the track. "Let us run with endurance the race God has set before us."

Picture for a minute you on a track. God is saying, "I don't want anybody coming into your lane to trip you up, because I have a race for you to run and I want you to run it with endurance. If you run this race I've called you to run, you're going to win a prize and you're going to be satisfied, because what I want to do in your life is better than anything you ever wanted to do in your life. So, I need you to trust Me. But there's something you've got to do—you've got to get all these weights off you!"

If you find a God-loving spouse who's a good match for

you, he can help you win the race of life God has put in front of you, and you can help him win his. But if the person you're dating is consistently weighing you down or holding you back now, he'll still be holding you back if you get married. Be patient and have grace, but if things don't change, you've got to go—better to call it off sooner than later.

Move out if your roommate is a bad influence. Drop the class if the professor is making you doubt your worth. Move on if your friend continues to stir up drama and gossip. Stay away if your teammate encourages you to lower your standards. And please don't put up with that boyfriend or girlfriend who hits you. End the relationship *now*.

Still not sure about some relationships, perhaps ones where it's more gray than black and white? Reluctant to pull the trigger and say it's over? Like always, the Word of God can help.

ABRAHAM AND HAGAR: TWO WAYS TO KNOW WHETHER A RELATIONSHIP OUGHT TO END

Abraham is the father of our faith. He wasn't perfect, but he was out there trying to obey God. One day (Genesis 15) God promised that Abraham would have a son. Abraham believed Him, but after that, years passed and both he and his wife, Sarah, got to be old. Like, really old. Like, dusty old.

Genesis 16 says Sarah got tired of waiting. She thought, *I'm old and dusty. Abe's old and dusty. I know I can't have no kids, but he might have a couple of swimmers left in there. Let me go ahead and hook him up with somebody younger I know has some childbearing hips and can get him his baby.*

So, she said to Abraham, "Well, the Lord has prevented me

from having children, so go and sleep with my servant, Hagar."

Abraham's eyes got big. He said, "Ah, ah, ah, you want me to do what?"

"You heard me, baby. Go sleep with Hagar. Perhaps you can have children through her."

Abraham said, "You know what? You are a smart one. I married me a smart lady."

(Or that's how I picture it going down.)

So, Abraham got Hagar pregnant, and she had a son— Ishmael. For a while, the situation was kind of awkward around the home, but eventually they all adapted.

More years passed. Abraham and Sarah got even older and dustier.

Yet in Genesis 21 we see that God's promise finally came true. Sarah was wrong when she'd thought the Lord was preventing her from having children; He'd just wanted her to wait. Now the gray-haired, seasoned Sarah gave birth to Isaac.

Hagar's boy, Ishmael, was a teenager by this point, and like some other teenage boys I've known, he got to be hard to handle. When Ishmael was teasing the new baby, Sarah raged. "Abe, you got to throw that woman and her troublemaking kid outta here. We don't need them anymore anyway. We've got Isaac. He's your heir."

Abraham decided he needed to pray on this.

God said, "Tell Sarah to shut up. You're not getting rid of your sidechick and your own firstborn. That's just mean." No, no, no, He didn't! Believe it or not, He said, "Go ahead and send them away. Even though you disobeyed, tried to get ahead of My timing, and didn't stay faithful to the instructions I gave you, it's cool. Both your boys are going to be okay because I'm going to take care of them."

All this shows us two of the most basic reasons for breaking up.

1. When You Realize That You Started It and God Didn't

God gave Abraham and Sarah a promise, but they started looking at their situation and wanted to "help" God do what He said He was going to do. All they really had to do was wait. Isaac was coming in God's time, but they ran out of patience and felt like they had to do something. That's when Sarah got her bright idea about Hagar, and Abraham went along without needing much persuasion and without consulting the Lord.

Isn't that how we usually get in bad romantic relationships? Instead of waiting for God to bring us the right person at the right time, we're *so ready* to have love that we go trying to fit somebody who is not right into the picture.

> YOU CAN'T JUMP-START GOD'S TIMING.

The same kind of thing can happen with friendships, roommate situations, and other relationships. Doesn't matter—you can't jump-start God's timing to do what He's going to do. All you can do is obey Him patiently.

When we don't wait on the Lord, we give the Enemy the chance to introduce us to counterfeits. Then we deal with the results of mistakes and have to get healed and delivered from something God never meant for us to experience.

I just want you to see that when you start relationships that God doesn't intend, it always ends badly for you (and for others!). Ishmael had nothing to do with the promise of a son that God had given Abraham. Abraham and Sarah's lack of patience not only caused themselves pain; it hurt everybody. Hagar, who was an obedient servant and ultimately driven out into the desert, and Ishmael, who, yes, was a punk as a kid but grew up fatherless, both suffered because of the impatient choices of others. There were negative ramifications all the way around. (Since the Jewish people are descendants of Isaac, and Muslim Arabs call themselves Ishmaelites, you could say that sibling rivalry is still going on today.)

If you're dating somebody, my question to you is, Are you starting this relationship just because you're impatient to be with somebody? Or do you have a real sense that God wants to bring this person into your life as part of His plan for you? If *you* started the relationship, not God, strip off the weight!

2. When the Relationship Is Picking on Your Promise

Ishmael was a product of impatience. If you think about it, Ishmael was not even supposed to be there, and when Sarah saw her son, the promised child, getting punked and bullied by the shortcut product of a relationship, she said, "They got to go."

In the same way, you might need to get indignant about relationships and people who have been stealing from you and punking you out of your promise, and you need to say, "You know what? I know we had a good thing for a while, but you got to go."

May I give you some practical examples? It's like, if you're in a relationship, and all that relationship is producing is lust, it starts bullying or picking on your purity. Purity is the promise that God has for you as a believer in Jesus Christ, but if your relationship is bullying your promise, it's time for that relationship to end. Or you may have a relationship with somebody who won't let you go and is monopolizing you. That relationship is producing isolation for you—it's keeping you from family, friends, church. Isolation is picking on the godly community God wants you to be in.

If you've been dating or engaged to somebody who won't let you be all that God wants, you got to let him go. God gave you promises for a reason. He wants you to have them.

BETTER EARLY THAN LATE, BETTER LATE THAN NEVER

Ben couldn't figure out why he wasn't happier after his girlfriend, Tina, accepted his ring and they started planning their wedding. It wasn't that he was too young for marriage; he was in his forties. And it wasn't that he didn't know Tina well enough; they'd been dating for five years.

Then Ben did something smart: he talked to a mentor, an older man from church. Having wise, mature people speak into our lives is more important than ever when the issue is a matter of the heart and we may not be seeing clearly.

Ben's mentor started probing, and soon he figured out some things. Ben had been deliberately ignoring some red flags in the relationship with Tina for years. Also, recently Tina had been pressuring him to get married. Ben felt guilty for holding her off so long, and he also thought he might be too old to find somebody else, so he proposed to Tina for time served, so to speak.

"What are the problems in this relationship from your perspective?" the mentor asked.

Ben thought about it. "One thing is, she wants all my time. I guess you'd say she's emotionally needy. I like to be with her, but she doesn't leave me enough time to do my business and other stuff I like.

"Another thing is that she doesn't like my friends. She wants us to hang out with her friends. Well, I really feel like I need my friends. Not only do I enjoy them, but they're the ones who keep me on the straight and narrow path."

At the mentor's advice, Ben had a talk with Tina and said they needed to put the engagement on hold while he thought some things through. Tina pitched a fit. You can imagine some of the words she threw at him. In the end she said, "Never mind. I'm outta here."

Today Ben is still single, but he's more content and productive than he has been in five years.

IS THIS RELATIONSHIP PUSHING ME AWAY FROM GOD OR TOWARD HIM?

What we can learn from Ben is that it's better to ask the question *Is this relationship pushing me away from God or toward Him?* earlier than later. The longer that relationship went on, the more damage it created for both Ben and Tina.

Even if we've waited longer than we should have to evaluate a relationship, it's better to do it today than tomorrow. Before the minister pronounces you married, it's not too late to reevaluate and, if it's necessary to break up, start on a better course.

If you're like Ben and you need to say it's over, what's the best way to go about it? Back to Abraham's dysfunctional family for insights . . .

ABRAHAM AND HAGAR: THREE QUALITIES
OF A GOOD BREAKUP

Father Abraham may not have been so wise in starting his relationship with Hagar in the first place, but when it came to ending it, he did it right. This whole part of the story happens in one verse, but it's a verse that can teach us a lot about how to break up: "Abraham got up early the next morning, prepared food and a container of water, and strapped them on Hagar's shoulders. Then he sent her away with their son" (Genesis 21:14).

1. End It Quickly

First, notice that "Abraham got up early the next morning." Now, if Abraham wasn't committed to ending the relationship like God had told him, he would have slept in that day. But God had agreed with Sarah's demand that Hagar and Ishmael should be sent away. So Abraham ended it quickly.

You might be hanging on to a relationship you know isn't good. You might be telling yourself it's worth trying to work things out. Or you might be waiting for the "right time" to end it. There will never be a right time. I'm telling you, you need to end it, and you need to end it fast.

2. End It Kindly

Abraham "prepared food and a container of water, and strapped them on Hagar's shoulders." He didn't even have a servant pack the supplies. He went and did it himself. He was going to end this relationship quickly, but he wasn't going to be mean and nasty about it. He was going to do it with bless-ings.

If the character of God is developing in you, then you should end a bad relationship generously, like Abraham. Even if she's done you wrong, even if she's bad-mouthed you to others, end it with blessing. Have a final talk for some closure. Give back the stuff she gave you. Be thankful and wish the other person well. The exception is if the situation has been abusive and a face-to-face breakup would be dangerous for you.

Romans 12:18 says, "If it is possible, as far as it depends on you, live at peace with everyone" (NIV). *If it is possible. As far as it depends on you.* Let's be honest—some people are crazy. If you're hooked up with somebody like that, then maybe it's better to send a text like "Don't ever call me again" and block him. But if you can be a blessing on the way out, do it.

3. End It Cleanly

"Then he sent her away with their son" (Genesis 21:14). I get the impression Abraham didn't stop to say, "Do you remem-ber when . . . ?" or "Oh, I don't know about this," or "Maybe it's just for a while." Abraham said, "You got to go." I bet that was hard, but Abraham ended it intentionally, defini-tively, cleanly.

Many people are ending relationships very vaguely. They're saying stuff like, "You know, it's just for the season. I just think we're supposed to take a break." That leaves an open door for people and issues to come back.

Remember, you're ending this relationship because it's rob-bing your promise and blocking your purpose. Don't go and be passive about this. You can be kind and still say clearly, "It's over. This is it. You've got to go."

BREAKING UP AIN'T THE HARDEST THING TO DO

I know you might think it's easy for me to say you should end a relationship. I don't know what that relationship means to you. I don't know what you and the other person have had together. You may be emotionally dependent or physically involved with the other person and feel like you can't give that up. You may be worried about whether anybody else is going to come along if you drop the one you're with. You certainly didn't start with the relationship goal of having it come to a painful end, and it feels like failure.

Well, let me go all pastor on you right now and reassure you: if the Lord wants you out of a relationship, He'll help you get through it. And there's something even bigger than that: *He'll bless you and bless the other person.*

Let me go back to Abraham and Hagar one last time. (Their story shows us that messed-up relationships weren't invented in this generation. They didn't even need social media to go wrong!)

When Sarah started hollering and yelling that Hagar and Ishmael had to go, "this upset Abraham very much because Ishmael was his son" (Genesis 21:11). Like, that sucks, because Hagar and Abraham held each other at night. They had something. It was easy for Sarah to say "Get her out of here," but she wasn't there when they were exchanging secrets. She probably wasn't there when he held Hagar's hand while she labored in giving birth to their shortcut child.

Abraham was saying, "Man, I got something with her. And her son is my son. This is hard!"

God got it. He told Abraham, "Do not be upset over the boy and your servant. Do whatever Sarah tells you, for Isaac is the son through whom your descendants will be counted. But I will also make a nation of the descendants of Hagar's son because he is your son, too" (verses 12–13).

Based on this, Abraham trusted God and went along with the plan.

When you know you need to end a relationship, you've got to trust God with it. Trust Him that you're going to be all right and the other person is going to be all right. He'll help both of you get over the heartache. And the only way either of you can proceed to your purposes in life is if this relationship comes to an end.

WHEN YOU NEED TO END A RELATIONSHIP, TRUST GOD WITH IT.

When you know God didn't start your relationship or it's picking on your promise, remember this about breaking up: everybody gets blessed. And if *that's* not enough, let me tell you: breaking up is easy to do compared to the alternative— living with the consequences of sticking it out in a relationship you shouldn't even be in.

6 SURRENDER YOUR SEXUALITY

Let's talk about sex, baby
Let's talk about you and me

—SALT-N-PEPA, "Let's Talk About Sex"

Mami, if he ain't rollin' with Christ
Then don't let him roll with you

—LECRAE, "Wait"

Sometimes it seems to me like, in our day, sex is as casual as saying hello or shaking somebody's hand. "You've been dating her for three weeks and you ain't hit it yet? What's wrong with you, bro?" "What do you want to do tonight? Do you want to catch a show or come over to my place and have sex?" This very, very common attitude devalues the power of sex, which is intended to intimately join people, not merely entertain. Sex was never meant as a leisure pastime for single people; it's a pleasure and purpose connection for married couples.

Yet married people aren't necessarily much different from singles when it comes to their looseness toward sex. You know as well as I do that on your job, and on your street, and more than likely even in your church there are married people planning hookups with others every day. A wife or husband doesn't seem to be enough for some people.

There are a lot of perversions going on too. You can be with two women at once, get your homeboy and have an orgy, touch yourself in front of a computer screen, sleep with a relative, or try to get away with molesting a child . . . And that's as far as I want to go with all that. It's heartbreaking. It's devastating. But it's real, isn't it? It's real and it's every day. Even when people don't actually do something, they still have perverse fantasies popping up in their minds.

What does all this sexual activity produce? Along with some brief pleasure, it brings devastation. Broken hearts. Divorce. Single-parent homes. Disease. Abuse. Inability to trust. Anxiety. Self-loathing. Isolation. Numbness. Coldness to God.

And people are taking their relationship goals from the society around them? Really?

Whether you're single or married, I know your sex life may not have been absolutely pure. Mine hasn't either, as I've already fessed up to you. I'm not here to come down on you, because the Holy Spirit and your own conscience can convict you better than I ever could. Instead, I want to share a Bible verse: "Do not let any part of your body become an instrument of evil to serve sin. Instead, give yourselves completely to God, for you were dead, but now you have new life. So use your whole body as an instrument to do what is right for the glory of God" (Romans 6:13).

> YOUR CREATOR GAVE YOUR BODY TO YOU; GIVE IT BACK TO HIM.

Do me a favor and read that verse again.

What that verse is talking about is surrender. Your Creator gave your body to you; give it back to Him. Male or female, married or unmarried, old or young, same-sex-attracted or opposite-sex-attracted, longtime Christian or just getting to know this Jesus thing . . . *surrender your sexuality to God.*

The world's idea about sex—do whatever seems fun for

you as long as it doesn't hurt anybody else and you can get away with it—is so common that it seems like it must be right. Sorry, it's a counterfeit. But if you're always buying knockoff Nikes, you get so accustomed to the cheap leather and the soles that fall out that when you see the real thing, it doesn't look right.

All I'm asking is, make the effort to start looking at sex God's way instead of society's way. It's not about what others think. It's not even about what *you* think. Get yourself to the point where you can surrender your sexuality to God. Because if you trust Him, He'll show you the truth about sex and help you "use your whole body as an instrument to do what is right for the glory of God." And that's a beautiful thing.

SEX IS GOD'S IDEA

To some people, it seems like Christians have so many rules on sex that God must hate sex. No, no, let me tell you, God is trying to help us enjoy sex the way it was intended. It's the Enemy who makes sex dirty. The Enemy's trick is to arouse a secretive sexual lifestyle at a young age, because then it's hidden and bad things can go on behind the scenes that we get a thrill from.

Maybe when you were a kid you watched movies you weren't old enough for, or you discovered porn, or some nasty-minded older kids gave you their version of sex ed, or a grown-up did something to you that was criminal. You were introduced to sex in a wrongful, hush-hush way, and you started certain habits. Now you've done it all these years with your girlfriends or your boyfriends and your friends with benefits and your big cousin that you hope ain't your big cousin.

Then maybe you get married. All of a sudden, sex is no longer so pleasing because it's not scratching the itch, because it's not a secret anymore. It was good when you weren't supposed do it, and now that you get it inside marriage, it no longer pleases you because it loses the air of secrecy and perversion. That's why a man will be in the closet masturbating even though he has a wife right there in the house to meet his need. He's driven by the rush of a secret.

The Enemy wants you to think sex has to be sneaky and transgressive, but the truth is . . . *sex is good*! Sex is God's idea. It's a gift from Him to us.

We have to redeem and reclaim this idea of sex.

What is the first statement that God said to Adam and Eve after their creation? First He blessed them. Then He said, "Be fruitful and multiply" (Genesis 1:28). Can I translate it for you? He says, "Y'all are blessed; go have sex. Do that thing. Put it down, Adam!" That's what my God said to Adam, okay? He wasn't talking about planting a tree to be fruitful. He told them to be fruitful *and multiply*.

And Adam and Eve were down with that. They got busy being "united into one" (2:24). I think we can assume a lot of one-fleshing was going on in Eden. And they didn't go hide in caves or behind trees to do it. They didn't feel it had to be secretive or saved for the dark of night. "The man and his wife were both naked, but they felt no shame" (verse 25).

What does this tell us? That God made us to enjoy sex if we do it in the right context.

I want you to realize this because, until you can acknowledge the fact that sex was created by God and that sex is good, your distorted idea of what sex is will always be preeminent in your mind. Of course there's such a thing as modesty or discretion, but sex is not something that we have to treat like a dirty thing. I have to reset this idea so that we can see sex how God sees it. So, say it with me: "Sex is good." Go ahead and say it again. "Sex is good." Now say, "Because sex was God's idea."

> **GOD MADE US TO ENJOY SEX IF WE DO IT IN THE RIGHT CONTEXT.**

Sex is about the coolest thing going when it's inside the context that God meant for it to be in. And not only is it cool; it's powerful. Really powerful. So powerful that it can take distinct qualities of two different people and join them together to create another life with a unique God-given DNA, personality, and purpose.

SEX CONTAINER

What is water when its full power is uncontained and on the loose? Hurricanes, floods. It's destruction. Or it leaks into where it's not supposed to be and causes rust, mildew, and rot.

But when water is properly contained and channeled, it can turn electrical turbines and provide light and power for an entire city. Sometimes it's carried as irrigation to where it can water dry soil and grow new life.

What does it look like when we're having sex outside marriage? It looks like destruction. It can get into areas of our lives that we never thought it could get into, weakening things or leaving a smelly residue.

Sex is not an abomination. Sex is amazing. But God put it in a container that is supposed to control it so that it can give Him glory. When it is out of that container, it becomes disruptive and creates death rather than life. I'm talking about spiritual death, emotional death, even death to our confidence and self-worth—not to mention missed opportunities, wasted time, and obsessive behavior.

And just to be totally clear: What is the sex container?

The covenant of marriage.

What does Jesus say about this? " 'God made them male and female' from the beginning of creation" (Mark 10:6). That means God knows our parts. He knows our desires. He knows our urges. He knows our appetite. He knows all of that, and how does He know it? Because He created us from the beginning; that's what it says.

Jesus goes on, "This explains why a man leaves his father and mother and is joined to his wife, and the two are united into one" (verses 7–8). The word *joined* is talking about sexual intimacy. And notice that it specifically says that in the plan of God, a man is joined "to his wife." (Same thing goes, of course, for a woman and her husband.) This lets you know that it's supposed to be in marriage. You're not supposed to be joined to that dude you work with or joined to that person you go to school with or joined to that person you met at the club and you aren't even sure she gave you her real name. You're supposed to be joined to your husband or to your wife.

When Jesus says "joined," the connotation of that word is so much more powerful in the original language than in today's. That word *joined* implies that the two really became one. They were joined spiritually, emotionally, and physically, which is what happens every time you have sex with somebody.

Jesus goes on and says, "Since they are no longer two but one, let no one split apart what God has joined together" (verses 8–9). There's the "one" and the "joined" again. He says it again since He knew some of us (like me) would be remedial and need to hear it again. Maybe He had an idea that people would need reminders that sex is intended for a lasting, covenantal marriage, not just for playing around. Maybe He knew it would be an ongoing temptation for cultures around

SEX IS INTENDED FOR COVENANTAL MARRIAGE, NOT FOR PLAYING AROUND.

the world and through the centuries to try to turn sex into something that is both secretive and heavily promoted, all at the same time.

"FREE" ISN'T ALWAYS FREE

I want us to get into the letter of 1 Corinthians, but first I need to fill in some backstory. When Paul wrote to the believers in Corinth, he was talking to people in a society that was a lot like ours today. This city in Greece had a temple that had about a thousand prostitutes working in it. Part of the "worship" there was to have sex with one of the prostitutes. And in general, this city was known for being a society full of lust. It was like the Las Vegas Strip of its time, catering to sinful impulses.

Paul was talking to believers who had come out of this lifestyle and were trying to live a Christian lifestyle. He was trying to give them practical steps to live spiritually in that kind of world, much like we have to do every day.

One thing he had to do was show them that sex outside marriage wasn't the casual, acceptable thing people thought.

Just like today, some Christians in Corinth were defending promiscuity on the basis of their freedom in Christ. "I am allowed to do anything," they said.

Here's Paul's response: "You say, 'I am allowed to do anything'—but not everything is good for you. And even though 'I am allowed to do anything,' I must not become a slave to anything" (6:12). In other words, even though some Corinthians thought they were exercising their Christian freedom by having sex with different people whenever they wanted, they were actually giving up their freedom. What's

GIVING OVER OUR TRANSGRESSION AND INIQUITY

Let me teach you two words for sin that are biblical and are totally real about our sexual immorality.

- *Transgression* is crossing the line, trespassing where God has said you shouldn't be. Example: breaking the commandment against adultery.

- *Iniquity* is a sinful desire in the heart. Example: being lustful.

One happens inside, and one happens outside.

Let me make it clear: it's all sin. Jesus said that if you even look on a woman lustfully, then as far as your guilt goes, you might as well have already committed adultery (MATTHEW 5:28).

But this is the most important thing about transgressions and iniquities—Jesus did something about them!

He was wounded for our transgressions,
He was bruised for our iniquities. (ISAIAH 53:5, NKJV)

sometimes called "sexual freedom" isn't free at all. It's actually slavery to sex. It's not a casual good; it's a serious harm.

This goes back to what I've been saying about how having bad relationships can punk your purpose. It isn't just about obeying rules. It's about doing things the way God intended, doing what's good for you, doing what advances you in God's plan. The Bible is telling us we shouldn't have anything that's a master over us except the Master.

> **"SEXUAL FREEDOM" IS ACTUALLY SLAVERY TO SEX.**

Look how beautifully all this fits together:

- *Transgressions* are the outward sinful actions. Where do you get wounded? On the outside. That's where Jesus was wounded for our transgressions.

- *Iniquity* is the inward sinful desire. Where do bruises form? On the inside. And that's where Jesus was bruised for our iniquities.

Jesus says to you, "I let them beat Me and whip Me and stick thorns in My scalp and lay a heavy cross on My shoulders and nail My hands and feet to that cross for a reason—so that you could walk in freedom. That's how much I love you."

As the verse from Isaiah goes on to say,

> The chastisement for our peace was upon Him,
> And by His stripes we are healed.

Say it to yourself: "I'm not the sexual sins I've committed. I'm not the bad thoughts I've had in my head. I'm not doomed to continue being immoral or struggling with guilt and shame. I'm not broken—I'm healed!"

You know you're maturing when you stop evaluating things by saying, *Is that a sin? Is that a sin? Is that a sin?* No. You're asking, *Is this making me more like Christ? Or am I a slave to this?*

Sex isn't the only issue here. Some people are slaves to others' opinions. Some people are slaves to video games. Some people are slaves to food, drink, or drugs. Some people are slaves to credit card companies. Some people are slaves to a job. Some people are slaves to their morning coffee from Starbucks.

But one of the worst things to be a slave to is sexual impurity. Let me tell you why: sexual impurity is one of those sins that doesn't come alone. In most cases, you can't be sexually impure and not be a liar. Just think about it. Let's say, back when you were in high school, you were heading out of the house one night to go meet your boyfriend or girlfriend for sex. Your dad stopped you on the way out and asked you, "Hey, what are you going to do tonight?" You wouldn't say, "I'm going to have sex. See you at eleven." No, you said, "We're going bowling." I'm just saying, you automatically learn to lie.

With sexual impurity comes deception. With sexual impurity comes manipulation. Sexual sin brings unbelief. It brings the whole party to your house. That's why the Enemy would love for you to keep secrets in those areas, because it invites in other things that you don't have power to keep out.

Even the Bible's King David: When he committed adultery, what's the first thing he did? He lied. And after he lied, he murdered. He was known as a man after God's own heart but still succumbed to the pull of secret sexual sin. Do you think you're exempt?

So, you thought you were just going to spend the night at

your girlfriend's. Or load up the porn again because it's the weekend and you don't have anything else to do. Or have a little rendezvous when you're out of town on business without your spouse. *No one will know, but it's exciting for me! It gets the adrenaline going! I might feel a little twinge of guilt, but after all, I'll tell myself that God doesn't really care about that stuff. He's got bigger issues on His mind than a little fooling around, which everybody does anyway. It's not going to do any harm. I'm a grown-up and not doing anything illegal with anybody who is not a "consenting adult"—so I can do what I want!*

And then you're entangled in immorality. You're covering up. It's changed how you think about yourself, others, and God. You're obsessing over getting caught—or over figuring out how to do it again as soon as possible. Suddenly this isn't freedom. You're enslaved to sexual immorality.

You start out saying *I'm allowed to do anything,* but then you end up feeling like *I don't want to, but I need that rush again* or *I'm so tired of this hollow pattern, but I feel compelled to try it again.*

So, you tell me: Is that really freedom?

NATURE THAT'S MORE THAN NATURE

In Corinth—the Las Vegas Strip of ancient Greece—some of the new Christians had another defense for sexual immorality. Not only did they claim spiritual freedom, but they also had an argument based on naturalism. It still sounds reasonable and practically scientific to a lot of people today.

People in Corinth were saying, "People have to have sex because our bodies have sex organs and we get horny, just like we have to have food because we have stomachs and get hungry. It's the same thing. It's just how our bodies work. It's natural."

Paul said it's *not* the same thing. "You say, 'Food was made for the stomach, and the stomach for food.' (This is true, though someday God will do away with both of them.) But you can't say that our bodies were made for sexual immorality. They were made for the Lord, and the Lord cares about our bodies" (1 Corinthians 6:13). In other words, Paul was saying that the whole food-sex comparison wasn't apples to apples.

> **THERE'S NO SEPARATING THE SEXUAL AND THE SPIRITUAL.**

Our sex organs were designed for sex in the right context, but not for sexual immorality. They were made for the Lord. There's no separating the sexual and the spiritual. Just forget that idea.

The implication is that while we should not be giving ourselves up as slaves to sex, we *should* be submitting our whole wills and minds and bodies to God. We should be surrendering ourselves to Him, who made our bodies *for Himself*.

I'm going to talk straight at you now.

Sis, you're not your body. You're more than that. God has made you special and beautiful, and these busters around you who just want you to send them pictures and do all this—they don't want you. They want what you can provide for them. Tell them to leave you alone, and one day you'll say (in the words of the "prophet" Beyoncé), "You turned out to be the best thing I never had."

Bro, it goes for you too. You're more than your body. If

you would think about your full worth in Christ and not be instructed by your other head, I believe God would use you. He would make you a man of valor, a man of honor, a man of stature. You can lead a wife and children. You can be a man who says, "As for me and my family, we will serve the LORD" (Joshua 24:15).

You can't be in sexual impurity and not be affected by it. God doesn't want you enslaved to sin; He wants you surrendered to His goodness. He's saying today, "You have to take this perverted view of sexuality that is breaking you, that has you looking at people distorted, that has you looking at yourself like you're not worthy—you have to give that back to Me and let Me redefine it. What I created sex to be is *good*. Who I created you to be is *good*. But what this thing is doing to you is *bad*! You got to let pornography go. You got to stop sexting. You got to stop this sliding into the DMs to set up your hookup. You got to stop letting people slip in and out of your bed, in and out of your heart. You got to stop giving away what belongs only to your wife or husband. You got to let Me have this, because I love you more than anybody else ever could."

LOSING PIECES OF HIMSELF

Patrick was like a lot of people: He saw sex in dating as normal. Sex was just a benefit that came along with being in a relationship, like having somebody to go to concerts or dinner with.

But over time, after he'd slept with a bunch of different women, he realized it was changing him. "I was losing pieces of myself," he told me. "Things that used to be important to me no longer gave me any joy. My passions were drying up. Somehow all the casual sex was making me numb."

He began to rethink his attitudes toward sex. He started praying, asking God to reveal to him how he needed to change in his relational life. Then one day he heard a preacher compare a person who has had a lot of sexual relationships to a box of chicken nuggets that has been passed around in a group of people that touch them, nibble them, and spit them out and still aren't satisfied. "Nobody wants to be the chicken nuggets that are left in the box after they've been handled by a bunch of others. They weren't created to be picked over. They were meant to be enjoyed."

It was kind of a silly analogy, but it got through to Patrick. "I flashed back on everything I'd ever done with women in bed," he said. "I decided, *From this day on, I will be faithful to purity until I marry.*" He doesn't want to be like picked-over food for his future wife and, more importantly, for himself. He knows he's more than that.

Patrick surrendered his sexuality to God.

Many of you can identify with Patrick, and others of you are in the middle of a situation like this. The comfort you have is that "if anyone is in Christ, he is a new creation; old things have passed away; behold, all things have become new" (2 Corinthians 5:17, NKJV). So, if you feel picked over, all you have to do is turn, or repent, and a new start is extended to you through the finished work of Jesus Christ.

REDISCOVERING EACH OTHER

Kimberly and Spencer were a married couple who viewed porn individually and together, and they didn't see anything wrong with this. When they had sex, both of them would replay pornographic scenes in their minds. They thought it brought some spice to the bed. But it meant that the other person wasn't much more than a performer playing a fantasy role. In fact, it was almost like the other person wasn't even there.

After they both found Christ, they started questioning the effect that porn was having in their relationship. They admitted that they were feeling disconnected from one another. Something that was supposed to unite them—sex—was driving them apart because of the borrowed images in their minds.

They asked for advice about this problem from an older couple at church. This other couple encouraged Spencer and Kimberly to commit to three months of not viewing porn as well as of deliberately trying to block out pornographic memories from their minds while having sex. Instead of acting out scenes, they would focus on being present with each other and loving and giving pleasure to each other. After three months, they should evaluate.

It didn't take that long. Immediately they started noticing a difference. After years of porn use, it wasn't easy to eliminate all those images from their minds, but to the extent that they did, it brought them closer.

"We realized we had to give porn up once and for all," said Spencer. "We turned our sex life and our thought lives over to God."

Kimberly and Spencer surrendered their sexuality to God.

WHAT ABOUT YOU?

Kimberly and Spencer, Patrick, and so many others have had fears and doubts and questions when they have surrendered themselves to God. But they have all found that surrendering themselves to the God who loves them wasn't a loss—it was a gain. If *you* surrender yourself to God, you can trust Him with your heart, your present, and your whole relational future.

Have you ever rented an apartment? The key to having a good rental experience is having a good landlord. If something breaks down, like the plumbing starts to leak, you're not responsible because you don't own it. You call the landlord, and this person comes over or sends somebody to take care of that drip under your sink.

First Corinthians 6:19 tells us that we are not our own. Our bodies are the temple of the Holy Spirit. That means we're not the owners, but many times we live our lives like we do own ourselves, especially in the area of sex.

In your sexual life, if you're not surrendered to God (the Landlord), there's not a lot of hope when you have problems and issues and urges you can't control. Your own wisdom and willpower only go so far. And if your sexual immorality has grown so strong that you're actually under the control of sex—you're its slave—then, frankly, you're doomed. If you've been fighting against a sexual habit or addiction in your own power and losing, then you know exactly what I mean. It's hopeless without a surrendering of ownership.

But if you've surrendered to God and He owns you, then He can come in and manage the problem.

See, you were bought with a high price. When God sent Jesus, that was the payment—the eternal payment—for God to own us, for Him to come in and be able to change us and have power over our situations. He said, "I sent My only Son because you were so important that I'd take care of this debt forever. Now you have a response. I need you to honor Me with your body. Don't do things or watch things or think things that would take you from the purpose that I have for you. You were bought with a high price. Honor Me with your body" (1 Corinthians 6:20).

So, my question is, Who owns you? Do you own you? Does your sexuality own you? Do society's ideas of sex and relationship own you? Does a lover own you? Does a relational memory own you? Does a relational dream or fantasy own you? Or does God own you?

Trust Him. Turn yourself over to Him, because God can manage only what He owns. God says, "Hey, I'm a good, good Father. If you give Me back what I gave you, I promise you, I'll bring management to what I

DOES YOUR SEXUALITY OWN YOU? OR DOES GOD OWN YOU?

own." There is nothing too big for our God to bring under the subjugation of His power, but He's not going to take it from you. You have to give it to Him.

TERMS OF SURRENDER

How do you need to surrender your sexuality? Let's look again at Romans 6:13: "Do not let any part of your body become an instrument of evil to serve sin. Instead, give yourselves completely to God, for you were dead, but now you have new life. So use your whole body as an instrument to do what is right for the glory of God."

Any part of your body. Your whole body. This gives us some clues about what we need to do. Our surrender needs to be comprehensive.

How about your **brain?** Have you been indulging in sexual

fantasies that you could never righteously fulfill in real life? Ask God to help you capture your own rebellious thoughts (2 Corinthians 10:5) and fill your mind with pure and honorable thoughts (Philippians 4:8).

How about your **eyes**? If you have a habit of staring at hot bodies and imagining things, ask God's help to get control of those eyes, because this is eyeball adultery (Matthew 5:28). Tell Him you need His help to stop ogling or to stop bringing up bad websites. He'll help you establish a covenant with your eyes (Job 31:1).

Or your **ears**? A lot of music lyrics today are immoral, and they arouse certain feelings and give you certain ideas. Ask God if you need to delete some songs from your music app and change your listening habits. Maybe it would help to fill your mind with hymns and spiritual songs (Ephesians 5:18–19).

Your **mouth**? Are you a sweet talker, a seducer? Or on the other hand, are you a dirty talker? Would God approve of everything that comes out of your mouth? Ask Him to help you change your speech so that you say nothing that leads you or anyone else to destruction (verse 4).

Your **thumbs and fingers**? Do you send sexts or type come-on texts? God can show you the bad habits you've gotten into. Ask Him if you need to take a season off Instagram and Facebook until you can form better habits (James 4:8).

I don't think I need to go any lower in the body than that because you can work out the rest yourself.

Seek God's help with prayer and fasting and Scripture to make any changes you need to in your sexual behavior. I'm not saying that surrendering to God will make all of this easy. But do it anyway. You may have to go up to your husband and say, "I've been emotionally cheating on you with somebody at the office, and today I've come clean because God only frees people in truth." You may have to tell the girlfriend you've been sleeping with, "It's over. I'm packing up and going." You may have to give somebody else permission to review

SURRENDER UNCONDITIONALLY. YOU WON'T BE SORRY.

your online history. Drastic measures may be called for (Matthew 5:29–30). It can be scary or embarrassing or saddening, but do it anyway. Surrender unconditionally.

You won't be sorry. If you acknowledge God as the owner of your sexuality and invite Him to come in and manage you, you'll start seeing positive changes. And you'll get back on track with your relationship goals.

TODAY IS THE FIRST DAY
OF THE REST OF YOUR SEX LIFE

If you're ready, make today a turning point in your sexual history. Drive in a stake. Put a big red X on the calendar for this date. Commit yourself to giving your sexuality to God by praying this prayer:

A Prayer of Sexual Surrender

God, I don't know how to do this on my own, so I'm giving You my sexuality. I have done things, said things, experienced things that I know were outside Your will for me. And today I'm asking You to take ownership. I want to live a life of value that is centered in Your love for me and not my desire for temporary fulfillment.

Reset my priorities to purity. Refocus my thoughts on faithfulness. Renew my mind with Your identity for me. Rebuild my self-worth until I truly believe I'm Your masterpiece. Realign my perspective to see myself and others the way You see us. Restore my broken pieces and make me new.

I give You permission to uproot my damaged areas of rejection, pain, hurt, shame, guilt, and bad examples that negatively shaped my perspective. And I'm asking for You to cultivate in me the fruits of the Spirit from Galatians 5 that will produce love, joy, peace, patience, kindness, goodness, faithfulness, gentleness, and self-control. I surrender my sexuality. I'm Yours.

In Jesus's name, amen.

Surrendering your sexuality will change your whole future. Why? Because while sexual immorality destroys purpose, getting back your purity restores your purpose. "If anyone cleanses himself . . . , he will be a vessel for honor, sanctified and useful for the Master, prepared for every good work" (2 Timothy 2:21, NKJV).

7 ALL TIED UP

I'll never give myself to another the way I gave it to you
You don't even recognize the ways you hurt me, do you?

—RIHANNA, "Rehab"

Get out of my head, get off of my bed
Yeah, that's what I said

—AVRIL LAVIGNE, "Don't Tell Me"

The marriage of Caleb and Chloe started out with all the hope and promise that most marriages do. But within weeks it blew up when Chloe found out that Caleb had just hooked up with his ex-girlfriend Jasmine.

Caleb and Chloe came to Natalie and me for counseling, so we listened as the whole story came out. It wasn't pretty. Caleb had been exposed to sex at an early age, and soon, in his mind, it seemed that the way to show someone he cared about her was to have sex with her. By the time he got married at age twenty-nine to Chloe, he'd had sex with countless other women.

His most recent girlfriend before Chloe was Jasmine. I asked him why he didn't break it off with Jasmine when he met and fell in love with Chloe—or at least when they got engaged.

"I knew I shouldn't still be with Jasmine," he explained. "And I guess that's why it was so exciting. Keeping that relationship going behind everybody's back was a rush."

He went on. "The other thing, and I know it sounds weird, is that I kind of talked myself into it. I mean, I would tell Jasmine stuff like 'We're perfect for each other,' even though we weren't. Or 'Nobody understands me like you do,' which wasn't true either. I heard these words from my own lips over and over again, and I started to believe it."

I helped Caleb see that what he was doing there was using his spoken expectations to reinforce his emotional entanglement with this woman. He had a strong lingering connection with her called a soul tie. In fact, in his case the soul tie was more like a bunch of ropes with knots binding him to Jasmine emotionally, physically, spiritually, and even verbally. A part of him wanted to get out of it, but he was stuck in a giant net. That's why he went back to Jasmine even after he was married.

Chloe separated from him, and the marriage quickly went to the brink of divorce. For a year and a half, it was bad—really bad. Nothing like what anybody wants their newlywed days to be like, I assure you. But during that time, Caleb finally broke off his relationship with Jasmine and began to undergo some real change. Trust is now entering back into the marriage. I occasionally see smiles on their lips like you'd expect between two people in love.

I don't know what the future holds for these two. They're still in marriage counseling every week and turning to God together, so I'm hopeful that they're going to make the marriage work. But who knows? The story isn't over.

Caleb and Chloe's relationship might be a win in the long run, but if so, it will be by winning ugly. The saddest thing is, all the pain they've been through wouldn't even have been necessary if Caleb had dealt with his soul ties *before* getting married.

SOUL TIES

The soul is made up of three distinct parts: the mind, the will, and the emotions. Your mind is how you think, your will is what you desire, and your emotions display how you feel. If you think about it, the collaboration of these three entities directs your entire life.

It's not surprising that what someone's soul is exposed to can be very influential in his life. Soul ties happen when someone allows his soul to become attached to someone or something that has the power to affect him. There are all kinds of soul ties: godly ones and ungodly ones, constructive ones and destructive ones.

Marriage is a godly soul tie. If you are married, God wants you and your husband or you and your wife to be connected on a soul level, satisfying each other spiritually, mentally, and emotionally and working to fulfill each other's desires for as long as you both shall live. We'll get a better picture of what this looks like in the next chapter when we look at what I call God's plan of oneness.

There are also friendship soul ties. David had that kind of tie with King Saul's son Jonathan: "There was an immediate bond between them" (1 Samuel 18:1). Jonathan had a son's loyalty to his father, but his soul tie with David was so strong that he stepped in to prevent Saul from killing David.

Other (hopefully positive) soul ties include your connection with your parents, siblings, and other relatives. The apostle Paul called Timothy his "true son in the faith" (1 Timothy 1:2) because he felt so tied to him as a spiritual father. The Bible tells us that members of the church are like family. Neighbors, coworkers, teammates, and others can form connections that are good for all involved.

But there are also ungodly soul ties—things that we attach to and that attach to us that negatively affect our purpose. You can see these ungodly ties in gang members, pimps and prostitutes, dealers and addicts, friends who are leading each other astray, abusive relationships, and false teachers who have congregations under their control.

You can even have a soul tie with a thing. What is alcohol or drug addiction besides a soul tie to a substance? And have you ever seen *Cast Away*? It's a great movie that paints a pretty bleak picture. Tom Hanks's character is stranded alone on an island, and his best friend becomes a volleyball named Wilson. This shows that attachments can form with anything, especially when you're desperate.

And then, of course, like Caleb and Jasmine, we can have soul ties with sexual partners outside marriage. This is one of the greatest means the Enemy has of blocking purpose and destroying lives.

I know that going to bed together can seem like no big deal, but what you may not know is that an invisible string forms a tight knot binding people together when they connect

GOING TO BED TOGETHER FORMS A TIGHT KNOT BINDING PEOPLE TOGETHER.

in this way. So, every time you get out of that bed belonging to a person you're not married to, it's not over when you leave the room. You've joined physically, and by default, your thoughts, emotions, and desires have become intertwined. Later on, feelings of guilt and shame might cloud your perception, and the same temptations and urges are bound to return.

Maybe you've had a lot of sex partners in your life and now are living with a whole bunch of soul ties with these

THE UNBREAKABLE TIE

The apostle Paul asks, "Can anything ever separate us from Christ's love? Does it mean he no longer loves us if we have trouble or calamity, or are persecuted, or hungry, or destitute, or in danger, or threatened with death?" (ROMANS 8:35). He could have said, "Does it mean He no longer loves us if we watch pornography, masturbate, fantasize, or have sex outside marriage?" The answer is still no. Of course God is always opposed to sin, and of course sin has its consequences, but still, if we are in Christ, *nothing separates us from His love!*

That's not because we love Him so much but because He loves us so much: "Overwhelming victory is ours through Christ, who loved us" (VERSE 37).

I don't know about you, but I am overwhelmed that—thanks to Christ—my mistakes and my missteps have not separated me from the love of God. I think Paul felt the same way.

I am convinced that nothing can ever separate us from God's love. Neither death nor life, neither angels nor demons, neither our fears for today nor our worries about tomorrow—not even the powers of hell can separate us from God's love. No power in the sky above or in the earth below—indeed, nothing in all creation will ever be able to separate us from the love of God that is revealed in Christ Jesus our Lord. (VERSES 38-39)

people. Think about what happens when you try to go after God's purpose for your life. All those strings are pulling and pulling. You've got all these ties holding you back.

Unrighteous relationships set you back in your relationship with God because sin creates separation. God doesn't want to be separated from His most valuable possession—you—but some things just don't mix. Light and darkness can't be in the same place at the same time, but then that's why He wants to come into the dark areas of your life and light them up.

Real talk here: Healing relational damage takes up your time and drains your energy. Ungodly soul ties can cause delayed destiny, wasted time, emotional stress, trust issues, bitterness, insecurities . . . and the list goes on. These, and so much more, are ways soul ties with ex-lovers can beat up on your purpose and put your future at risk. Unhealthy soul ties are always easier to create than break.

Remember what I was saying in chapter 5 about a runner being slowed down by weights? This is exactly what I was talking about. Can you imagine trying to run a race while being tied to someone else who's running in the opposite direction? I imagine the two of you wouldn't get very far very fast, and you'd probably exhaust yourselves trying.

The concept of soul ties is one that not many people understand, yet it's a reality. And it's one of the biggest reasons why we don't achieve the relationship goals that God wants for us. The illegitimate soul ties from the past are hindering us, and we need to learn how to cut them and get free if we're going to make progress toward our aims.

Soul ties can be persistent, but they don't have to be permanent. The Holy Spirit can help you break unhealthy ties that are slowing you down and distracting you from godly purpose. If you want a strong soul tie in marriage, then you've got to do what Caleb is doing—break off the soul ties from past partners. The same goes with other bad soul ties from other kinds of relationships. You can identify them and disentangle them one by one. But remember, it's the soul ties formed by sexual immorality that can be the most harmful when you consider the entire relational progression of your life. This, I'm afraid, is serious stuff.

I'm going to go out on a limb here (even though I don't think it's really much of a limb at all): even if you're single, in a way, you have "married" everybody you've had sex with. Dare me to prove it to you?

MARRIAGE WITHOUT COVENANT

Let's go back to the passage of Scripture we started looking at in the previous chapter: 1 Corinthians 6. Paul says,

> Do you not know that your bodies are members of Christ himself? Shall I then take the members of Christ and unite them with a prostitute? Never! Do you not know that he who unites himself with a prostitute is one with her in body? For it is said, "The two will become one flesh." But whoever is united with the Lord is one with him in spirit. (verses 15–17, NIV)

Some of the new believers in Corinth were going to the temple prostitutes, arguing that their Christian freedom allowed them to do so and that sex was just a natural function their bodies needed, like eating. But look at the Old Testament verse Paul threw at them: "The two will become one flesh," from Genesis 2:24. This is the same verse that talks about a man leaving his parents and becoming joined to his wife. We have applied that verse to marriage, but as we see here, Paul applied it to a casual sex event!

Casual sex is also cause-ual sex—it causes a bond to be created.

God has made sex so powerful that every time you have sex with somebody, you are not just joining physically through that action; you are joining emotionally through the intimacy created, and you are joining spiritually because you are two people each with a spiritual nature inside you. So, this is why I say that every time you have sex, you're "marrying" somebody, just without the covenant. A connection is formed, a strong soul tie.

Here's the reason why if you had sex with somebody before you got married and that person walked into the room right now, you'd be all jacked up. Maybe it's been fifteen years since you've seen her, but there's still a soul tie connecting you to her, and now it's invading your thoughts and emotions with memories. Maybe you thought it was one night that you would forget, but God says you "married" that person without the covenant.

MAYBE YOU THOUGHT IT WAS ONE NIGHT THAT YOU WOULD FORGET, BUT...

If you study the Scriptures all the way from the Old Testament to the New, you'll see that blood always had to be shed to legitimize a covenant. *Warning:* If blood makes you queasy, just stick with me through the next few examples and I promise you'll be okay. For Abraham, there was a bunch of cut-up animals (probably would have made some good barbecue!). The ancient Israelites sacrificed animals at the temple altar. And of course our Lord's blood dripped down the cross for you and me.

Now, I'm pretty sure this is something you weren't taught in high school sex ed, but think about this: when a woman loses her virginity, blood is shed. It's supposed to happen when she gets married. It's supposed to be a sign of a covenant of marriage being fulfilled. But when a boyfriend takes her virginity while they're dating, her blood is a sign that a false covenant has been created. The same soul-tie thing happens every time either one of them has sex outside marriage: each one is making a counterfeit marriage through sex.

Did you know that biblically speaking a couple is not considered officially married when they put a ring on it, say yes to a dress, find an elaborate location to spend way too much on a bunch of people that they probably don't even like, say "I do" and kiss at an altar, get rice thrown at them, cue fireworks, and . . . okay, maybe I'm ranting now. But the point is, back in the day, signing a piece of paper didn't mean you were married. These are all things from our modern culture and law.

Biblically, a couple were married when they consummated the relationship physically. God recognized a marriage was real when a man and a woman had sex. That made the covenant official.

The problem is, today most people are having sex without any intention of covenant. Yet they're "married" in almost every other way. My question is, How many people are *you* one with? How many invisible soul ties are connecting you to other people?

NO CONDOM FOR YOUR HEART

The reason why it's so important for you to understand the power of even so-called casual sex is because there's no condom for your heart. You might be able to protect your physical body against things that can be transmitted sexually, but what about things that are transmitted *spiritually*? The Bible says it like this: "What do you benefit if you gain the whole world but lose your own soul? Is anything worth more than your soul?" (Matthew 16:26).

People tend to think that protecting your body is enough. The socially acceptable thing to do is have "safe sex," but what many fail to realize is that wrapping it up covers only one area . . . and even that isn't totally reliable! I've counseled and dialogued with thousands of people who were practicing what they believed to be safe sex but still ended up with broken hearts, broken spirits, and broken relationships, and they found that trying to put those pieces back together wasn't worth the moment of pleasure they had experienced.

All right, let's take a break from all the heavy stuff and go to something lighter. This may be a little corny, but I'm writing this book while simultaneously helping my daughter Bella with her kindergarten homework, and we've been working on using acronyms to help us remember important things.

So, let's see if this one helps you. The only way to practice SAFE sex is within the sex container: the covenant of marriage.

S is for *sacred*. There's a reverence for something that is sacred. It's considered holy, set apart, and not just frivolously given away. It holds great weight and great worth. Most of all, it's connected and dedicated to God.

A is for *anointed*. Don't get all churchy on me. If something is anointed, that just means it has God's stamp of approval, and God loves sex! He created it Himself and thinks it's awesome as long as it's happening between a married man and woman.

F is for *faithful*. Now, I could go in a million different directions with this one, but the number one thing I want you to remember is that God remains faithful to us, so we should strive to remain faithful to Him and reciprocate that character to those we commit to in relationship.

E is for *exclusive*. This one's pretty simple. Sex should be between one man and one woman. Oh yeah, sorry— I keep getting ahead of myself. I said I was going to talk about that in the chapter on God's plan of oneness. Stay tuned!

There's no condom for your heart. That may be a bit of an extreme example, but I want you to realize that your heart is so important to God. Having sex outside marriage affects the core of your being, and there's nothing you can do to stop it. When you are in covenant, this connection forms a godly soul tie and produces beautiful intimacy, but when you're not, it produces dangerous detours.

> **HAVING SEX OUTSIDE MARRIAGE AFFECTS THE CORE OF YOUR BEING.**

I challenge you to allow God to help you guard your heart and soul by abstaining from sex outside the container He designed. A proverb we've already looked at applies perfectly here:

> Guard your heart above all else,
>   for it determines the course of your life.
>   (Proverbs 4:23)

Now, I can pretty much guarantee that if you haven't practiced SAFE sex, you have experienced the symptoms of soul ties. To take the analogy a step further, you could be having a "heart attack." You hear a song, and in your head you go back to the place where you had your first dance with an old lover. An ex-girlfriend used to wear Sweet Pea from Bath & Body Works, and when you smell that fragrance, mentally you're back with her. Maybe when you're disappointed in your husband, you find yourself scrolling down a social media page and daydreaming about what life would be like for you if you'd stayed with that other guy who was so charming and so good in bed.

It's not that you have some kind of unusual obsession. It's just that it's never easy to separate two people who have been sexually intimate. It's like if you glue two pieces of paper together, let the glue dry, and then try to rip the pieces of paper apart. It's messy. It's damaging. Remember, your hearts are involved, so in terms of emotion, you're going to have pieces of the other person stuck to you, and the other person is going to have pieces of you stuck to him.

Does any of this sound familiar?

- "We split up, but we have a kid together and that will always keep us connected."
- "We split up, but I'm always thinking of you."
- "We split up at my insistence, but you're stalking me."
- "We split up, but I still get jealous when I see you living life without me."
- "We split up, but now I've got to get in touch with you because I just got a medical diagnosis that may have something to do with you."
- "We split up, but you hurt me so bad that I'm clinically depressed and in need of counseling."
- "We split up, but I gave you a piece of me that I should have saved."

- "We split up, but you had anger issues and now, for some reason, I find myself getting mad all the time."
- "We split up, but things we did in our past are still creating trust issues in my present relationships."
- "We split up, and now you're telling your friends everything we ever did, and it's humiliating."
- "We split up, and now I see how stupid it was to get together with you in the first place, so I don't trust my own judgment anymore."
- "We split up, but while I was with you, I stopped going to church or praying or reading the Bible, and now I feel like God doesn't want me."
- "We split up, but I invested so much in you that I don't even know who I am anymore."

How many of us are walking around with pieces of us torn off, so we can't be who we should be in marriage, parenting, business, ministry, and other areas of our lives? Isn't it easy to see how soul ties distract us from doing the things we're meant for and get in the way of our pursuing the relationships we want?

I wish I could say that type of interference in our progress in life is the worst thing about forming unrighteous soul ties. But I've got to tell you the truth: there's something even more heinous to think about.

IN BED . . . WITH JESUS

Once we accept Jesus as our Savior, we've formed the most important, positive soul tie we could have. As I said back in chapter 2 and keep repeating, this is our ultimate relationship, and cultivating it should be our number one relationship goal, no matter where we're headed or whom else we've got in our lives. And Paul confirms this connection with God when he says, "Do you not know that your bodies are members of Christ himself?" and "Whoever is united with the Lord is one with him in spirit" (1 Corinthians 6:15–17, NIV).

What that means is God is not watching what we're doing from a camera, like Big Brother, observing, evaluating at a distance, perhaps averting His eyes at embarrassing moments. No, He's right here with us, taking part in everything we do. So, if we're forming or strengthening harmful soul ties with other people, then we need to know it's pulling on our soul tie with Christ.

Let me be clear: sex outside marriage not only violates the relationship we're supposed to exclusively have with our spouse; even worse, it violates our relationship with the Lord. This is where Paul got really upset: "Shall I then take the members of Christ and unite them with a prostitute? Never!" (verse 15, NIV). That sounds seriously angry to me.

This wasn't an urgent situation only for the Corinthians. If you're in Christ, it's an urgent warning for you too:

- If you're pulling over to pick up a hooker, Christ is a part of the solicitation.
- If you're having sex with a gf/bf or a friend with benefits, you've taken Christ with you into that bed for sex.
- If you're sleeping with someone who is married but not to you, Christ is right there with you as you defile the marriage bed.
- If you're watching porn, Christ is sitting beside you, and the reflections from the screen are hitting His face.

- If you're engaging in some kind of perversity, Christ knows exactly how you're distorting His design for creation.
- If you're taking advantage of someone who's too weak, too young, too drunk or drugged, or too mentally limited to consent to sex, Christ is there for the assault.

This goes with other kinds of ungodly soul ties besides sexual ones as well. If your business partner proposes a way of hiding income from the IRS and you go along with it, Christ is there for the cheating. If your friends are bullying somebody and you decide to take the easy route and join in, Christ is in the crowd as you're tearing down the victim's self-worth.

The acts themselves are wrong. Involving the holy Lord in them is worse.

I want you to remember this for the rest of your life. The next time you get ready to send private pictures to somebody, or the next time you get ready to slide into the DMs or lie in the bed of somebody who's not your husband or wife, I want you to realize that *you cannot separate sex and Savior.* Christ will be there.

If you're a believer, your unity with Christ is a permanent thing; it doesn't come and go. It's just a fact for you. So, now it's a stewardship issue. How are you going to handle Christ in you?

For many years, I devalued Christ in me. I took Him to places He shouldn't have ever been. We watched things together we should never have seen. I regretfully violated the creation in front of the Creator. I've confessed, and it's been forgiven by God's grace, but sadly I can't undo what I did.

You might want to think about it like this: When you're having a good time in bed with somebody you're not married to, is God having as much fun as you are? Is He as comfortable in that position as you? Christ is not enjoying it; He's just enduring it. United to you out of love to redeem you from the very brokenness you're creating.

> **WHEN YOU'RE HAVING A GOOD TIME IN BED, IS GOD HAVING AS MUCH FUN AS YOU ARE?**

If you're not motivated to break your unhealthy soul ties for your own sake or the sake of your loved ones, do it for Christ.

CUT IT

Is this idea of soul ties making sense to you? Are you saying, "Yup, I've got a nasty ol', dirty ol' soul tie with that person and that person and—oh yeah—that person"? More importantly, what are you going to do about these soul ties?

The best thing is not to create a soul tie in the first place. Don't even get into a relationship where it is going to tie you up and hold you back and pull you down. If you have not gotten into an ungodly soul tie, good for you. The grass is not greener on the other side. There's actually a desert over there. But if you have already stepped into a dangerous relationship, just get out of that situation as fast as possible. That's what Paul says: "Run from sexual sin!" (1 Corinthians 6:18).

Run. Not walk. Not stand there pondering what to do. Not toy around with sin a little and try to see how far you can take it before you really get in trouble and have to react. *Run* from sexual sin.

Running is what you do when you're threatened. If someone was armed and came into a room filled with people and started to shoot, everybody would run and scatter. Everyone would get out of that place immediately and ask questions only later. In the same way, sexual sin is an assault weapon to your purpose, and you need to break it off immediately so that you suffer as little damage as possible.

> **SEXUAL SIN IS AN ASSAULT WEAPON TO YOUR PURPOSE.**

For you, *running* might mean saying no to a date offer you just got from that guy who's smokin' hot and a gentleman but is up front about how he is not a believer. Or it might be putting some boundaries in place with your girlfriend because your date-night activities are about to cross a serious physical line. I know a guy who gave away a brand-new Mac laptop just because he was ready to run from porn. (I know, you're thinking, *Couldn't he have given it to me?*)

If you're currently involved with someone who's standing in the way of your purpose and involving you in stuff Christ doesn't want to be a part of, running means running away from the relationship. You need to end it. Like we said earlier, do it quickly, do it kindly, do it cleanly, but do it.

Unfortunately, it's easier to break up with a person than it is to get rid of the invisible ties that may still be attached between you and someone else. You'll never be able to change the fact that you were once physically united with a person in your past, maybe many persons. Your heart and your spirit were affected by the experience.

So, after the running comes the cutting. Cut those entangling strings, those soul ties. Here's how you do it.

Call It

The first thing you have to do is to *call it*. I mean, call it what
it is. Don't romanticize and act like it was the best thing that
ever happened to you. It's been robbing you. You need to call
it what it is: a thief (aka soul tie). Thieves are not friends.

Confess It

Then you need to *confess it*. God can't heal what you won't
reveal. Many people aren't self-aware, or they live in denial.
Calling it to yourself is one thing, but confessing it to someone else is another thing. This can be to a counselor, a friend,
your spouse, or a trusted mentor. The same way that we are
damaged by relationships, we heal in relationships. I know
you might feel apprehension about sharing with others, but
this is the antidote that James prescribes: "Confess your sins
to each other and pray for each other so that you may be
healed. The earnest prayer of a righteous person has great
power and produces wonderful results" (James 5:16).

Cancel It

The next step is to *cancel it*. When a television network realizes it has a bad sitcom on its hands, it cancels the show and
removes all signs that it ever existed. No commercials adver-
tising it, no reminders of what was. Like that, you can get rid
of everything that reminds you of the soul tie. Get rid of the
necklace he got you, the Jordans she bought you, the tablet
you're reading this book on . . . well, at least after you finish
the book. This probably is the most inconvenient step to cutting the soul tie, because you might have to change your num-

ber, move locations, find a new job, attend a different church, change your cell-phone plan, or find a new friend group. You might be thinking, *It don't take all that.* My question is, How long do you want to be trapped?

Cast It

After you call it, confess it, and cancel it, you need to *cast it.* This is not the time to be ashamed, downtrodden, or despairing. Nor is it the time to act like nothing happened or that it doesn't hurt. This is the time when you throw the weight that you can't carry onto the One who can. "Cast all your anxiety on him because he cares for you" (1 Peter 5:7, NIV).

The comfort that you have from cutting a soul tie is that God cares. He really cares. He's not standing in heaven saying, "I told you so." He's right there with you, cheering you on. He's proud of you. And now you've given Him permission to empower you to live a better life, a life free from harmful soul ties.

One of the many definitions of *cast* is "to throw off." When we cast our cares, that practically means that we throw off our concerns to God through prayer. Don't think prayer is something that you need the right mood for, you need to light candles for, or you have to be holier-than-thou to do. Prayer is just talking to God. Tell Him honestly how you feel and what you need from Him. "Let us come boldly to the throne of our gracious God. There we will receive his mercy, and we will find grace to help us when we need it most" (Hebrews 4:16).

· · ·

This has been a heavy chapter. Well, actually, it's been a truthful chapter about a heavy topic. So, I want to end with some encouragement: The practical steps I've given you to break soul ties are only one side of it. There's also God's side.

LEVERAGING YOUR SOUL TIE WITH CHRIST

Calling it, confessing it, canceling it, casting it—all that is good for cutting your unwanted soul ties. But when you're dealing with something as powerful as sex, I've gotta tell you—it's not enough. It's like someone on a diet. He eats quinoa and drinks green tea for three weeks, but then he falls off the diet because good intentions aren't enough to get him through. You know what I mean?

Maybe you're saying, "I see what you're saying about breaking ties with our past sexual sins and resuming our relational progress in a pure way. I'd like to. But it's so hard. I'm single and I can't live without sex." Or "I can't get these perverted thoughts out of my head. I know because I've tried." Or "She doesn't want me anymore, but I really love her, and the way I feel about her is the only connection I've got left with her." Or "I'm addicted to the porn now. I can't stop." Or "My boyfriend doesn't want to get married, and I can't leave him because we've got these kids."

You're right—you can't fully break soul ties on your own. But God in you *can*!

Remember, your number one soul tie is with God. Leverage your unity with Him, and seek His power. It's explosive power. Death-defying power.

Just after Paul said, "The body . . . is not meant for sexual immorality but for the Lord, and the Lord for the body," he added something that might seem out of place. He said, "By his power God raised the Lord from the dead, and he will raise us also" (1 Corinthians 6:13–14, NIV).

That really messed with me when I first saw that. It's a beautiful thing and I believe it, but why would Paul say that right here? Why did he choose to mention resurrection power when he's talking about sexual immorality?

I thought about it and thought about it . . . and finally I got it.

Paul knew the readers of his letters—those Corinthians from a sexually immoral culture like ours—would feel discouraged about what he was saying. They would think it was too hard, if not impossible, to abandon all sex outside marriage. There were too many temptations, too many habits, too strong of an inner drive to overcome. So, Paul was saying, "I don't care what your sexual problem is right now. If God has the power to raise Jesus's body and later raise your body from the dead, then He has enough power to help you manage your body while you're living!"

You may not be able to get your improper sexual habits under control, but God can get them under control for you if you allow Him.

As we surrender our sexuality to God, He is not just going to leave us there and be like, "All right, figure it out for yourself from here on out." No. He says, "I'm the God with all power. What I came to do is support, restore, and strengthen you. With Me inside you because of My Son and through My Spirit, you have all the power you need to break every soul tie that is holding you back from the relationship goals I've inspired in you."

Maybe you've already tried and tried and tried to break your soul ties. Maybe you've already thought of the practical

MAYBE YOU'VE TRIED TO BREAK YOUR SOUL TIES. BUT HAVE YOU TRIED JESUS?

advice that I gave you above, and you tried to put it into practice. You tried. But have you tried Jesus?

Sex has power—*but God has more power!* Your unwanted soul tie is not too strong. It is no match for the power of God in your life.

8 THE TRIANGLE

We had to learn how to bend . . .
I had to learn what I've got, and what I'm not, and who I am

—JASON MRAZ, "I Won't Give Up"

Forever can never be long enough for me
To feel like I've had long enough with you

—TRAIN, "Marry Me"

Ever since you walked right in, the circle's been complete

—BOB DYLAN, "Wedding Song"

I bet you played house when you were a little kid. Maybe you or your friend had the new Barbie and Ken dolls, and you pretended they were happily married, living their best life together in Barbie's DreamHouse with the rooftop swimming pool and the pink convertible parked out front.

The real thing isn't quite the same, is it?

Don't get me wrong. Marriage is amazing . . . when you marry the right person, when you *are* the right person, when you're committed to working on issues, when you learn to apologize for eating her leftover takeout, when you don't get offended as she keeps telling you to put the toilet seat down. (Sorry, Natalie! I think I'm talking about my issues.) All I'm trying to say is, a marriage is only as good as the individuals in it.

But there's even more than that to a great marriage, the kind of marriage anybody would want in relationship goals. See, I used to assume that two people who are each at about 50 percent come together, and in combination they make 100 percent or as close to it as they can get. It even seemed biblical because, as we've seen more than once, we're told, "A man leaves his father and mother and is joined to his wife, and the two are united into one" (Genesis 2:24). In other words, I thought the marriage equation was $\frac{1}{2} + \frac{1}{2} = 1$. In my mind, that was why people call their spouses "my other half" and say things like "You complete me."

Jerry Maguire is such a liar.

I've been married for some years now, but I realized early on that my original marriage equation was all wrong. The equation for marriage is really this: $1 + 1 + 1 = 1$.

Are you currently questioning everything you learned in second-grade math class? Let me help you. One whole man plus one whole woman plus God in their midst creates one healthy marriage.

If you're married, it's important for your marriage that you've been working on yourself before and during the relationship progression. Hopefully your spouse has been doing the same. But even more important is the presence of the third partner in the marriage. God's participation in the marriage makes it possible for the husband to fulfill his purposes, for the wife to fulfill her purposes, and for the marriage to fulfill its purposes.

Let me propose that this verse should be required reading at every Christian wedding: "Make every effort to keep yourselves united in the Spirit, binding yourselves together with peace" (Ephesians 4:3). We should be seeing to it that God is at the center of our marriage relationship, enabling both partners to grow closer to one another and to Him while at the same time fulfilling our purposes as individuals. And if a relationship like that endures for a lifetime, it's not too long.

DRAWING CLOSER

I'm not the first to say it, but it's true: A godly marriage is like a triangle. First, the husband and wife are connected at the bottom of the triangle. When this is done in marriage, this is a beautiful connection, an honored connection, one that is intended to bring life to both people. This isn't an entangling tie that has to be painstakingly and painfully severed, like you get when two people have sex without marriage. From day one of their marriage, a wife and husband are bound together in a holy covenant, a soul tie of an awesome sort. The bond is intended to last for a lifetime, and they will hopefully be strengthening their connection and enjoying the rewards of it for as long as they live.

But there's another part of the triangle. God is at the top, with each of the marriage partners spiritually connected to Him (assuming they're both believers in Jesus). This gives them another way to be connected—through God. And look at this: it's a geometric and spiritual truth that as each partner draws closer to God, each one is also drawing closer to the other. The fact that God is in the middle of that marriage is the key to their getting the relationship win.

GOD IN THE MIDDLE OF MARRIAGE IS THE KEY TO GETTING THE RELATIONSHIP WIN.

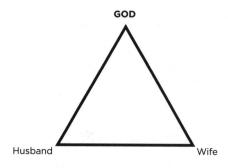

Let me point out another truth the triangle can show us: a triangle is not a pulley system. What I mean is, if the wife thinks she's more spiritual and a more faithful Christian than her husband, she can't pull him up. (And of course the opposite is true as well: he can't pull her up.) Take *Fixer Upper,* for example. It's a great show! Fixing up works on houses because most aspects are within your power to influence and you don't usually have to dig far below the surface. Not so much on marriage relationships, at least within the bounds of your own power. Even though the partners may be at different places in their spiritual progress, it's not a competition against one another. It's not "I'm closer to God than you. I pray more. I know more about the Bible. I don't have those sins you do. So, let me show you where you're failing." No, God is responsible for lifting both partners up toward Him, together, hand in hand, and He does it gradually, in His own way, over time.

Even though you're bonded in marriage from the day you say "I do," becoming one with your marriage partner is a lifetime process. Drawing nearer to God is a lifetime process too. These are marathons you run as each other's cheerleaders, not as competitors.

GOD'S PLAN OF ONENESS

Can I give you what I call God's plan of oneness? He wanted it to be one God, one man, one woman, one marriage, one sex partner, one flesh, one lifetime to create one picture. It's a whole lot simpler, stabler, and more beautiful than all the crazy, messed-up ways people do relationships in our culture. It's all about oneness.

But wait—what do I mean by "one picture"?

Marriage is supposed to be a reflection on the earth of the relationship God has with the church: "As the Scriptures say, 'A man leaves his father and mother and is joined to his wife, and the two are united into one.' This is a great mystery, but it is an illustration of the way Christ and the church are one" (Ephesians 5:31–32).

> **MARRIAGE IS A REFLECTION OF THE RELATIONSHIP GOD HAS WITH THE CHURCH.**

A lot of people say things like this: "I've never seen God. I can't believe in God." They need something to help them grasp what it's like to be in relationship with the invisible God.

I believe that was behind God's intention for marriage—that people who don't know Him would see a healthy marriage and would say, "Oh, I'm beginning to understand God's love for us now." And they would seek God at the same time they seek righteous relationships with other people.

Most of us can't afford to have an expensive painting, like one by Monet or Renoir or somebody like that. So, companies make copies, or reproductions, of paintings like that for us. A lot of us, in our houses or apartments or dorm rooms, have a print like this on display. It's just a copy, but it's beautiful because it looks like the real thing and points back to the real thing.

That's what marriage is like. The real thing—the one-of-a-kind masterpiece—is God's relationship with His people. But a godly marriage is a beautiful copy we can all look at and admire. And what it reveals is an image of faithful, sacrificial love.

Marriage was never supposed to be just a husband and wife. God was always supposed to be a participant in the relationship. In fact, He's supposed to be the focus of the relationship. That's because God is love, and love has an action that goes with it. We all know the scripture "For God so loved" that He did what? "He gave." John 3:16. You will never see real love until there's real sacrifice of giving.

Most people in our age want to take. They may not always say that out loud, but in their hearts they're wondering, *What can I get out of this relationship? What's in it for me?* You may have been hurt by this attitude in someone else, or you may have done the hurting.

The real mark of love is giving, and giving takes sacrifice. That's why Ephesians 5:25 says this for husbands: "Love your wives, just as Christ loved the church. He gave up his life for her." And wives are to submit to their husbands (verse 22). This is not aggressive, authoritarian dominance. This is having a vision and being "sub" to that mission. That's why I like to call this loving submission; it looks like what Ephesians 5:21 says for both the husband and the wife—to "submit to one another."

You want a real definition of marriage? It's gonna be a lot of dying to self. You're gonna wake up every morning and you're gonna die to yourself. What you want to do, your likes, your hopes for the day—you're going to have to put some of them on hold for the sake of your spouse. But it's all for unity, and it's one of the most beautiful pictures, because you become more like God and can give to somebody who doesn't want everything that you want.

God's purpose for your marriage is that you as a couple win in relationship. But it isn't a selfish grab kind of thing. I don't want anybody to go into marriage thinking it's not gonna be how Jesus said it was; namely, that you will love your spouse sacrificially. This is why I said back at the beginning of the book that love, in the fullest sense, doesn't really come until after marriage.

FIRST COMES MARRIAGE, THEN COMES LOVE

Our culture—you know, the one that screws up relationships so badly for us—emphasizes love *before* marriage. Think about all the love songs, the rom-com movies, the TV shows, the ads . . .

Meeting somebody we like can definitely stir up strong emotions real quick. But a lot of times those emotions come because we want to be in love and to have a relationship so badly that we've just attached somebody to our dream. The emotions blind us so that we can't even see the other person clearly. We don't know who they really are, and we may not be acting like our real selves either. They may be right for us, or they may not. Feelings alone are not enough to help us discern.

And then sometimes we think we're in love but we're really in something else that's called by another four-letter word starting with *l*: *lust*. You know what I'm talking about.

If you're dating and you feel like you're in love, I'm happy for you. It's a beautiful time that you'll look back on with fondness if the two of you wind up getting married. I'm just saying that when you're in marriage and committed to each other for life, you will discover a fuller, more mature kind of love—one that isn't all caught up in her looks and his sense of humor and having fun and cuddling but realizes just how much you have to give to each other.

WHEN YOU'RE COMMITTED TO EACH OTHER FOR LIFE, YOU WILL DISCOVER A FULLER KIND OF LOVE.

I've got a comparison that may help this make sense to you. How much did you love God before you accepted Him as your Lord and Savior? Really, think about it. Most of us didn't learn to love God until after we got in covenant with Him. Once we got in covenant with Him by His grace, then we started to progress in our relationship of walking in love with Him.

So, I just suggest to you that romantic love really gets solidified and really becomes real after you get married. It's created and forged over time, through highs and lows.

First Corinthians 13 shows us how: Love is patient and kind. *I've told you how to work that remote a thousand times, but that's all right; I'll explain it again.* Love is not jealous. *I don't mind that you make more money than I do. I'm proud of you, sweetheart.* Love is not boastful or proud. *Secretly, I know that I'm a way better cook than you, but I can just keep that to myself and eat your tough beef.* Love is not rude. *Just because we're together all the time, I won't let that be an excuse to stop noticing you and treating you with respect.* Love does not demand its own way. *I'd rather go to the beach for this vacation, but I can see how important it is for you to visit your parents, so Pittsburgh it is.* Love is not irritable. *You left your whiskers in the sink after shaving again, even though I've told you that grosses me out. But I guess you just forgot, so I'll clean up the mess myself.* Love keeps no record of being wronged. *You apologized; I accepted; it's over.* Love does not rejoice about injustice but rejoices whenever the truth wins out. *You were right and I was wrong. I'm glad we're on the same side again.* Love never gives up, never loses faith, is always hopeful, and endures through every circumstance. *No matter what challenges come into our lives, we will face them together with faith in God, and anniversary after anniversary, our life together will write a more heroic story.*

But it's not just that marriage *demands* more love. Marriage also *provides* more love. Real love comes after we're married because it can.

In marriage, we're *committed* to each other. We're looking at this as a lifelong deal, so we're going to be transparent on the deepest level two humans can get to, we're going to keep turning to each other, and we're going to serve each other. We're going to share our bed, our dreams, our kids, our hardships, our successes, our faith, our aging.

Earlier I emphasized that marriage is the God-ordained sex container because it keeps sex from spilling over its banks and causing a flood of destruction. But marriage is also the sex container because it's the most powerful act for keeping a couple really bonded to each other. An ongoing sex life brings a husband and wife back to each other in the most vulnerable and private way. It restores and strengthens their unity again and again and again.

And then, remember, God is the third partner in the marriage. His love is an infinite resource that He shares with us.

We sacrifice for our spouse in marriage, even though that's an unnatural act for selfish human beings, because God gives us the love to be able to do it. First John 4:19 is never truer than within marriage: "We love each other because he loved us first."

Over time, in a marriage, a couple's love grows to be more like God's, or at least that's what it's intended to do. (You know I'm talking about the ideal in all this, right? About the potential in this God-designed relationship? There's also the reality of two sinful people living in a sinful world, so no marriage looks like it should all the time.) And out of this love, they are ready to have children, if that's a part of God's calling for them.

FRUITFUL AND MULTIPLYING

One of Adam and Eve's first instructions was to be fruitful and multiply. This was not an agricultural command. This was a Marvin Gaye, turn-out-the-lights, let's-get-it-on type of command. For every action, there is a reaction, and sometimes it comes nine months later.

Children are a blessing from God, but many times the environment that they're born into is not healthy. I'm not talking about the living conditions or organic baby food. I'm talking about the real motivation behind their parents' multiplying. I counsel a lot of people who are parents because the individuals they're in relationship with won't pay attention to them. Their desperation for affirmation, attention, love, and appreciation leads them to have children in hopes that the babies will fill their emptiness. This type of thinking leads to tons of disappointment and unspoken expectations. A child can never fill the void created by an unresponsive significant other.

Other people have babies just because they're having sex and not taking precautions. A child shows up unintentionally. If the parenting this child receives turns out to be as careless and unplanned as his conception, that's not going to be the best situation for him.

These days, kids are growing up in one-parent homes where they get only half the adult gender modeling they need. Or their parents are living together but aren't married, and the kids grow up feeling vulnerable because they know that the foundation of the family—the parents' relationship—is based on an unofficial agreement that could vanish in a moment at one person's whim. Or the parents *do* get married for the sake of their child, but they don't really want to be married, so it's more of a duty arrangement and maybe the home is a place of conflict and resentment. Or the parents are divorced and the kids get volleyed back and forth between homes like a tennis ball. Or they're living with Mom because Baby Daddy is AWOL, but there's a succession of men coming through the home, putting the kids at risk and teaching them that it's normal for adult relationships to be temporary. Are we being honest with ourselves about what our relationships are doing to our kids?

The adult relationships in the home matter because kids can drink only from the well that is in that house. One generation's bad relationships beget the next generation's bad—or worse—relationships.

Now, I know we all make mistakes. And I know some people are single parents who never asked to be in that position.

UNITY AND DIVERSITY IN MARRIAGE

Even in a good marriage, the relationship can still be filled with tension—we're united in covenant, but it doesn't always *feel* like we're united. We're one and we're bound together, but we're also two and we're different.

It helps to remember that this tension is a lot like the tension between unity and diversity within the church, the body of people who are in a covenant of saving faith with Jesus Christ. Read Ephesians 4:3-8:

> Make every effort to keep yourselves united in the Spirit, binding yourselves together with peace. For there is one body and one Spirit, just as you have been called to one glorious hope for the future.
>
> There is one Lord, one faith, one baptism,
> one God and Father of all,
> who is over all, in all, and living through all.
>
> However, he has given each one of us a special gift through the generosity of Christ. That is why the Scriptures say,
>
> "When he ascended to the heights,
> he led a crowd of captives
> and gave gifts to his people."

Did you see? In those words to the church, the word *one* is repeated. But we also see that God gives different gifts to different people, which must mean He expects them to do different things for Him.

What if you asked God to turn your marriage tension into *creative tension*—true covenantal unity held in balance with your own God-given individuality and your spouse's? That sounds like a lifelong adventure right there!

Besides, people can change, and God can bring good things out of bad in totally amazing ways. But hear me: God's ideal is that we should reproduce out of our love, not out of our dysfunction. Our fruitfulness is supposed to be a part of our fidelity, and our multiplying is supposed to take place within marriage. The marriage triangle gives the best chance to create a safe place for kids to grow up healthy and positive until they're ready to go out into the world on their own.

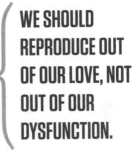

WE SHOULD REPRODUCE OUT OF OUR LOVE, NOT OUT OF OUR DYSFUNCTION.

Maybe you were not raised in that kind of home yourself. You're a child of divorce or of unmarried parents, with bad home examples from Mom and Dad, your aunties and uncles and cousins, and the grandparents. You probably grew up with some level of abuse or neglect, fear or anxiety as a result. Well, somebody in your family has to stand up and break the generational curse. Why not *you*? Declare today, "It's not going to be the same way with me! I'm going to have kids only within a marriage, one that honors God and lives out Christlike love."

That's a countercultural decision in our day, and I respect you for rising to the challenge. Meanwhile, another challenge you may have to deal with is sharing a life, and maybe kids, with someone who isn't a believer like you.

AN INCOMPLETE TRIANGLE

When I discussed dating in chapter 4, I talked about not being "unequally yoked" (2 Corinthians 6:14, NKJV). A believer shouldn't date a nonbeliever since a person who doesn't know

Jesus fails God's mateability standard, and the whole point of intentional dating is finding a mate who can unite with us in God's purposes and blessing, making a triangle.

WHAT IF YOU FIND YOURSELF MARRIED TO AN UNBELIEVER?

But what if, somehow, you find yourself married to an unbeliever anyway? It happens. I call this the incomplete triangle because the husband and wife are connected to each other but only one spouse is connected to God.

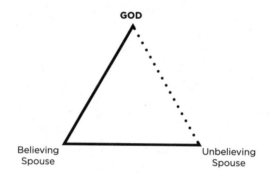

GOD

Believing
Spouse

Unbelieving
Spouse

It's not easy to be in an unequally yoked marriage. You love your wife or husband, and you want her or him to know the joy of being united with God like you do. Yet your spouse doesn't really want to pray or come to church with you or have a relationship with God. Differences of beliefs and values can lead to hurt on both sides and drive a couple apart. If that's your situation, I'm sure that negotiating the complexities of a spiritually mixed marriage was never a part of your relationship goals.

But be encouraged. The Bible talks about how the faith of one person in the household can save the entire family.

If a fellow believer has a wife who is not a believer and she is willing to continue living with him, he must not leave her. And if a believing woman has a husband who is not a believer and he is willing to continue living with her, she must not leave him. For the believing wife brings holiness to her marriage, and the believing husband brings holiness to his marriage. Otherwise, your children would not be holy, but now they are holy. (But if the husband or wife who isn't a believer insists on leaving, let them go. In such cases the believing husband or wife is no longer bound to the other, for God has called you to live in peace.) Don't you wives realize that your husbands might be saved because of you? And don't you husbands realize that your wives might be saved because of you? (1 Corinthians 7:12–16)

You may be in a place right now where you're thinking, *I wish I would have had relationship with God seventeen years ago when I married Joseph. Now it's painfully clear that we're in two different places.* Or, *I thought Amy was a believer like me when we got married. Man, I was so wrong.* Life might be complicated. There are strains. You don't feel like you're heading in the same direction all the time.

At the end of the day, though, God is a redeemer. He can take things that are broken and put them back together. He can fill in the missing side of the triangle. You can start again, and God can do something awesome.

In the meantime . . .

• Keep working on your own relationship with God. He must continue to come first for you no matter what.
• Try to understand your spouse's views on God, faith, church, the Bible, and so on. Maybe she has been hurt or has misunderstood something, and you can help.

- Accept that you can't force your spouse to believe. You can only encourage and be an example and a model of faith.
- Continue to love and try to build up your spouse, looking for the good in him.
- Avoid getting judgmental or acting superior. Stay humble.
- Negotiate issues like church attendance, moral standards, and parenting strategies with your spouse.
- Keep praying for your spouse, and ask others to pray too. Never stop believing God can soften the hardest heart.

Brian and Sheila got married young, had kids young, and had the added honor and burden of being a military family. At one point, their faith in God was strong, firm, and aligned, but several years later Brian started to drift away. Slowly but surely, he became more passionate about things they didn't agree on. It seemed strange to Sheila that he was so against the standards they had set together. Brian's decision led him down a dark path, and he decided that being separate was better than living together. He and Sheila were unequally yoked.

Despite his opposing actions, Sheila courageously decided to continue to pursue her relationship with God, teach their kids the standard of the Word of God, and love and pray for her husband. This was conflicting for Sheila because the unity they once shared seemed like a distant memory. Yet years of faithfulness were fueled by Sheila's relationship with God.

Eventually, she stumbled upon the *Relationship Goals* sermon series on YouTube. This gave her an extra boost to believe. She sent a video to Brian and asked him to watch it. This one seemingly minor act was the beginning of restoration in their marriage. Sheila's commitment to the covenant allowed Brian to have a change of heart. Today they are back together as a family, enjoying love and life and a restored triangle.

Sadly, though, some other triangles fall apart and are never restored.

A BROKEN TRIANGLE

When it comes to marriage, God's plan is to unite and conquer; Satan's plan is to divide and conquer. Have you ever noticed that the serpent didn't appear in Eden until *after* Eve had been created and there was unity between her and Adam? The Enemy saw a beautiful triangle of love going on, and in his wicked mind he decided, *I can't have this unity thing. I need to deceive.*

GOD'S PLAN IS TO UNITE AND CONQUER; SATAN'S PLAN IS TO DIVIDE AND CONQUER.

The Enemy still loves to see marriages falling apart. He hates God, and he doesn't want the world exposed to a representation of Christ's gracious love for His people.

Just imagine if someone took a Sharpie and scribbled all over the copy of the *Mona Lisa* or *Starry Night* by van Gogh or the Michael Jordan six rings poster or whatever you've got hanging up in your home. It would be a ruin, a desecration to your home decor. That's what the Enemy tries to do to marriage. He can't break up the unity between Christ and the church (the original artwork), so he tries to break up its image in the world (the copy)—the connection between the husband and wife. Then the whole picture seems to change. The marriage creates the opposite impression that it's supposed to—

people see a failed marriage and say, "See, love is impossible in this world."

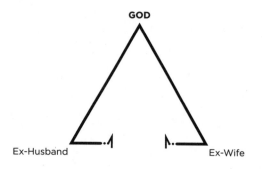

GOD

Ex-Husband   Ex-Wife

Satan loves divorce. But what does God say about it? "I hate divorce! . . . To divorce your wife is to overwhelm her with cruelty" (Malachi 2:16). Jesus said divorce "was not what God had originally intended," meaning the intent of marriage is lifelong unity (Matthew 19:8). He also clearly stated, "Since they are no longer two but one, let no one split apart what God has joined together" (Mark 10:8–9).

Jesus gave just one acceptable reason for divorce: adultery. "Whoever divorces his wife and marries someone else commits adultery—unless his wife has been unfaithful" (Matthew 19:9). We saw that sex is so powerful that even without a covenant it can create a kind of "marriage"; apparently sex is also so powerful that when one spouse goes outside marriage to get it, this can be a legit basis for ending the marriage.

Not that it *has* to end the marriage. Adultery doesn't necessarily mean the doom of a marriage. There are such things as forgiveness and reconciliation and restoration. (Thank God that Jesus doesn't divorce His bride for all our betrayals! Even if we are unfaithful, He remains faithful.) You and I have both known examples of marriages that have survived adultery. Divorce is not required in cases of adultery; it is just the most extreme allowable response for this sin.

Not being happy in the marriage is not an adequate reason for divorce. Wanting to marry somebody else is not an adequate reason either. Even being unequally yoked is an inadequate reason, although—besides adultery—the only other exception that the New Testament gives for divorce is when the unbelieving spouse in a Christian / non-Christian marriage wants to split up (1 Corinthians 7:15). The call for believers in a dysfunctional marriage is to stick it out and make it work as best they can.

I don't know what every person's relationship looks like. And there are probably nuances in your specific situation that are almost unbearable. But I urge you to really try for reconciliation if possible. If you are in an unhealthy, abusive marriage, get help. Don't suffer in silence. Maybe you need to separate and get intensive counseling. I have seen and counseled marriages that have been at this fragile place and been restored.

I don't take unhappy marriages lightly. The pain is often intense, and while you're dealing with the problems of the marriage, you're getting distracted from your personal purposes and goals. A big reason why I wrote *Relationship Goals* is because I desperately want people to make good marriage choices in the first place and avoid pain and frustration. But still, the marriage bond is so important that God does not want it broken except in the case of unfaithfulness. And besides, as painful as a bad marriage can be, divorce can be worse.

We talked about how a breakup between a dating couple who have been having sex is like ripping apart two pieces of paper that have been glued together. It's the same thing, only worse, in divorce. You've been glued together so thoroughly and so long and in such a meaningful, covenantal way that the damage that comes from pulling apart from one another is terrible. You're bound to leave big pieces of yourselves on each other.

I'd go so far as to say that going through a divorce can be worse than losing a loved one to death. Why? Because when somebody dies, there's closure. You bury her. You grieve. You learn to go on without her. But with divorce, it's a perpetual loss. Every time you see your ex, it can bring back the emotions and the regret. *I can't believe I wasted all that time on her.* Or, *There she is sitting with her new guy, and here I am alone. I'm such a loser.* There's squabbling over alimony and property and visitation rights. Your arguments were never really resolved; the covenant was just dissolved.

If you're in a dysfunctional marriage where no adultery is involved but you're tired of trying to make it work, I can confidently give you the command of the Lord: hold hands tighter with Jesus and try again at reconciliation in your marriage. Stop thinking of divorce as your out. If it helps, remember that many people who get divorced realize they're no happier than they were in the troubled marriage. Many married couples who have stuck it out through hard times have realized that the real gold came later.

If you're already divorced, well, then . . . what's done is done. Accept the new life and hope God is offering you today as a single person. I've already said it: there's nothing wrong with the single life. You can pick up your pursuit of purpose after divorce. And if you're thinking about marrying again, be twice as deliberate about it as a young person who was never married. The divorce statistics for second marriages are even worse than for first marriages. So be humble and realize that just because you've been married before, it doesn't mean you know everything and can wing it. This time around, be thoughtful, stay deep in prayer, and do whatever it takes to create a marriage triangle that will last.

Whether married and happy, married and struggling, single and satisfied, or single and looking, life goes on. And so do our relationship with God and His purposes for us. I want to especially show you what this looks like for a person who is married.

TO GO FORWARD, GO BACK

Some people get married and love each other and maybe have kids, and they think that's it. The end of the relational road. There are no more relationship goals to pursue because they've already arrived.

And maybe that attitude works, sort of, kind of, at least for a while. For example, until the kids are gone.

Why is the divorce rate for people over forty-five increasing? Because when the kids move out, too many couples find out that the project they had in common is gone too. I'm not helping with homework and taking Junior to the store to get some new Js. You're not packing lunches and driving to cheerleading practice. Now when I come home, I've got to look at you. We've got to talk. But we don't want to because the relationship ain't really there anymore. It vanished somewhere along the way when we stopped paying attention to it.

Do you remember the normal relationship process I laid out early in the book? **Singleness**, then **dating**, then **engagement**, then **marriage**, then **love** and maybe **children**, right? Well, when you're married, sometimes you need to go back to the beginning of the process. Yes, you need to be single and date again.

What?!

Naw, I don't want you to get a divorce and start playing the field. You know better than that by now. But listen to what I'm about to say because it's a key to keeping your marriage joy giving and God honoring till death do you part.

Even when you're married, you should never stop being "single." What I'm talking about here is being an individual and pursuing the godly purpose and goals you have for yourself, personally. Remember 1 + 1 + 1. You've got to keep working on your 1.

What's the point of finding a marriage partner who will support your purpose if you aren't going to go after it when you're married? Some people who are dating get too comfortable and stop thinking about their purpose, and the same thing can happen in marriage; it's a mistake either way. In marriage, you sacrifice your selfish desires for your spouse, but you don't give up your God-given purpose. Keep that godly drive burning.

So, let me ask you, What's the last thing you did to improve yourself? Did you go back and take a finance course so you can stack up the green better? Did you break a bad habit, like smoking? Did you make a fitness plan and stick to it? Did you decide to watch less TV and read one book a week? Did you study French so when you go to Paris you'll be able to tell whether they're serving you good food or not?

Doing stuff like this isn't selfish. It adds to the marriage. (You're taking your spouse with you to France, aren't you?)

Many people stop perfecting who God's created them to be because they joined with somebody else. That's laziness. That's lack of vision. Don't you do that. As a married person, keep working on your "singleness."

And then if your marriage is gonna last and be vibrant and have passion, keep dating. You know, *intentionally* dating.

When was the last time you took your wife or your husband out on a date? What that does is keep the relationship fresh. Don't just be with your mate, chillin' in the bed, watching movies. What happened to the pursuit? What happened to showing interest? Finding out more about each other? Connecting? Intentional dates between a married couple are a time for you to talk about things you might not talk about while you're busy taking care of business in your everyday lives.

But there's more. The thing about married dates that's different from single dates is, it's okay if they end up in bed. In fact, that's the best kind of married dates. You should be having a lot of those!

You'll keep changing as you grow older. So will your mate. You'll have new dreams and goals. So will your mate. You chose this mate because you believed he or she would be a godly support, and both of you need a marriage that continues to be mutually supportive, with or without kids in the house. So, keep going through the process. Work on your singleness, and date the one you love throughout your marriage.

> **WORK ON YOUR SINGLENESS, AND DATE THROUGHOUT YOUR MARRIAGE.**

ONE

If you're married, I hope you're building a relationship and a family of great beauty with your spouse. If you're single, I hope you're on track to be married to someone who loves Jesus like you do. Many of my greatest joys have come from my marriage with Natalie, and the same can be true for yours.

It's absolutely true that no human relationship, even marriage, can take the place of our relationship with God—but it's also true that no human relationship provides a better reflection of our relationship with God than marriage does.

Let's make this easy for you to remember. A triangle has three points, and remember that the equation is $1 + 1 + 1 = 1$. In a marriage, God wants us to become ONE.

O Means We Must Acknowledge *Ownership*

God is the owner of our relationship. He is the solid rock on which we build our marriage. I suggest that you and your spouse say this out loud: "God is the owner of our relationship." It may seem trivial at first, but life and death are in the power of your tongue.

After you acknowledge God's ownership in the marriage, you have to acknowledge the part that you own. God clearly defines the roles of a husband and a wife in His Word. Let these verses, which we've already touched on, guide you in their entirety.

Submit to one another out of reverence for Christ.

For wives, this means submit to your husbands as to the Lord. For a husband is the head of his wife as Christ is the head of the church. He is the Savior of his body, the church. As the church submits to Christ, so you wives should submit to your husbands in everything.

For husbands, this means love your wives, just as Christ loved the church. He gave up his life for her to make her holy and clean, washed by the cleansing of God's word. He did this to present her to himself as a glorious church without a spot or wrinkle or any other blemish. Instead, she will be holy and without fault. In the same way, husbands ought to love their wives as they love their own bodies. For a man who loves his wife actually shows love for himself. No one hates his own body but feeds and cares for it, just as Christ cares for the church. And we are members of his body.

As the Scriptures say, "A man leaves his father and mother and is joined to his wife, and the two are united into one." This is a great mystery, but it is an illustration of the way Christ and the church are one. So again I say, each man must love his wife as he loves himself, and the wife must respect her husband. (Ephesians 5:21–33)

N Stands for *Nurture*

We need to spend time praying, worshipping, serving, and giving because that nurtures, or cultivates, our relationship with God. At the same time, we have to nurture our relationship with our spouse. This is when we spend time praying for our spouse, serve our spouse, express our love to our spouse, and give generously to our spouse.

E Stands for *Evolve*

Evolving requires growth. Growth requires change. So, as you discover more about God and more about your spouse, it's inevitable for you to evolve or change. Pursue growth in both your relationship with God and your relationship with your spouse.

Remember the goal is to become ONE—one with God and one with your spouse to create one picture of heaven on earth. If that's not a relationship goal worth devoting your life to, I don't know what is.

9 MAJOR KEYS TO SUCCESSFUL MARRIAGE

Meet me at the altar in your white dress

—JAGGED EDGE, "Let's Get Married"

I got them keys, keys, keys

—DJ KHALED, "I Got the Keys"

I love this part of the book because this is where we get to do it together. The previous eight chapters of the book, you heard from me, but now I want to introduce you to the best part of my life—Natalie.

Say hi, Nat!

Hey, guys!

She's my high school sweetheart, the mother of all my kids. She's fine and she's all mine. She is the love of my life. I'm obsessed with her.

Boy, stop. But seriously, guys, I hope by this time in the book you're starting to take aim in your relationships, and I'm excited that we get to give you some serious, usable advice for marriage in the real world.

The reason we're calling this chapter "Major Keys to Successful Marriage" is because a key gives access to something that once was locked. This chapter has the potential to unlock everyone, no matter where you are in life. If you're single, you will be more equipped to value your singleness. If you're dating or engaged, it will show you things to prepare for and help you prevent some relationship problems you might face in the future. If you're married, it will take your marriage to the next level or at least be a good tune-up.

As Michael wrote in the previous chapter, marriage is the reflection of Christ's relationship to His bride, the church. I agree with him on that and honestly think that God's intent is for people to see Him through us in marriage. In other words, our marriage should be a reflection of God. What a huge privilege!

But don't get it twisted: Marriage is also dirty laundry, car repairs, bill paying, crying babies, stopped-up toilets, calendar syncing, meal prep, and the stomach flu. And it's misunderstandings, arguments, compromise, hurt feelings, and difficult reconciliations.

Would you agree, Michael?

Yes, totally.

MARRIAGE IS A PARADOX

Can we all agree that a healthy marriage is one of the most attractive things on earth? We love Denzel and Pauletta Washington, Tom Brady and Gisele Bündchen, Tom Hanks and Rita Wilson, LeBron and Savannah James, Fred and Wilma Flintstone . . . Well, maybe that last one is a stretch. But for some reason, everyone is attracted to that bond of marriage. That's why some people will fail at it eight times and still try for it (see Elizabeth Taylor).

Marriage is a paradox. It's the most appealing relationship on earth, but it requires consistent hard work and sacrifice.

MARRIAGE IS THE MOST APPEALING RELATIONSHIP ON EARTH, BUT IT REQUIRES HARD WORK AND SACRIFICE.

It's kind of like being fit. The definition of toned arms, chiseled abs, and strong legs is appealing to everybody. But let's just pause and look at ourselves . . . Just kidding! Kind of. That type of body is appealing but takes hard work.

Marriage is hard work too.

Building your dream home with the love of your life is appealing, but agreeing on location, decor, and budget is not easy. Who would've thought picking between marble and granite countertops would make you seriously consider becoming a nun?

For so many, having children is appealing. It's dreams of playing dress-up, cheering at Little League games, and throwing amazing birthday parties that make people want to have children. But things like infertility, special needs children, and even the death of a child are hard storms that marriages may have to weather.

It's appealing to think you have a best friend—someone whom you confide in where both of you have each other's back. But working through the emotional unfaithfulness of a spouse is hard work. Really hard work.

The power of this paradox shows that God is real. He can take two contrary qualities—and I dare say two contrary people—and weave them together into a beautiful tapestry that allows you and others to see God's craftsmanship. As I think about it, it's what He likes to do.

He asked a man named Moses with a stuttering problem to speak to the most powerful dictator at the time, Pharaoh. Paradox.

David, a shepherd boy with no formal training, defeated the giant Goliath. Paradox.

Sarah had a baby at ninety years old, when her husband was one hundred. Paradox.

Paul, a Christian-killer, became an apostle and wrote a large portion of the New Testament. Paradox.

The greatest paradox of all time is how Jesus, our Lord and Savior, died a gruesome death on the cross to show His love for people who may not even accept Him. Paradox. But because of this paradox, we have the opportunity to experience forgiveness, to extend forgiveness to others, to heal from our past, and to win in relationships.

With Christ's help, there are practical things we can do, habits we can form, to raise our marriages to the level where they're supposed to be—to get them to a point where they really do reflect (even though imperfectly) the relationship Jesus has with the church. Here are the Big Three.

🔑 KEY 1: UNDERSTANDING EACH OTHER'S NEEDS

What were you doing at twelve years old? Me—I was probably up to no good. But I remember hearing a song on 106.9 K-Hits that I didn't completely understand at the time. Over two decades later, including a decade of marriage, I'm finally starting to understand it. On November 28, 1999, Christina Aguilera released a hit song called "What a Girl Wants." The catchy, slightly annoying chorus of the song said,

And I'm thankin' you for knowing exactly
What a girl wants, what a girl needs

I wish that figuring out what a girl wants was as simple as this song. But I'm here to tell you that it's not.

And for us girls, the same goes for figuring out what a guy wants.

So, let us try to save you some time. A *want* is a desire for something or is something wished for. A *need* is a requirement that is absolutely necessary. In marriage it is crucial to know the difference between what your spouse wants and what your spouse needs. The sad truth is that the lack of understanding in this area leads to so much turmoil and unnecessary pain. If you don't know the needs of your spouse, neglect is inevitable.

DOES A FLOWER WANT WATER OR NEED WATER?

Many times we confuse a need for a want. Does a flower want water or need water? Does a car want gas or need gas? What we're going to list below are *needs* that men and women have. We don't give these things when we feel the other person has earned them. We don't give them as if they are bonuses. We give them because the other person needs them.

("Major key alert!" in my DJ Khaled voice.)

Men and women are equal in marriage, but God created us with different sets of needs. He designed marriage to allow the husband and the wife to fulfill those needs.

Instead of *me* telling you about all of it—Nat, will you tell the fellas what women really need and how husbands can meet those needs?

Okay. The information contained in the next few pages of this book could drastically change your life. Not only am I a woman, but I've also talked to many women, young and old, black and white. These three things seem to be consistently a necessity for their health and happiness.

Women Need Security

When I say *security,* I mean a safe place. A safe place for her emotional, physical, and financial well-being. Husband out there, your wife must find you a safe place for her dreams, her heart, her insecurities, her failures, and her feelings.

Creating an emotional safe place for her includes offering both trust and commitment on your part. A physically safe place is a place where she feels protected. This is super practical, but this includes a home and reliable transportation—even how you respect her body and her things.

The last place of security a woman needs is in finances. Now, for all my fellas still on the come up, don't trip. Every woman doesn't need you to be a baller, but she needs you to have a vision and a plan. Remember, when Adam found Eve, he had been given a vision by God and was working the plan. (In other words, ladies, if he's lazy and doesn't have a job, in the words of Queen Bey, "to the left, to the left.")

Women Need Affection

By *affection,* I'm not talking about sex. Sex can be a result of affection, but it should not be the motivation. More than likely, being affectionate is something you did while dating your wife. You probably took her out to eat, bought her gifts, and just wanted to be in her presence. Affection is one way to show your desire for oneness with her.

Story time!

As you know, Mike and I have been together for a long time. When we were younger, he would always do so many random things, like buy me some of my favorite gifts unexpectedly, write me letters, make me songs, bring something up to my workplace, remember anniversaries of sentimental moments. Those are things that I'll never forget.

In the beginning, affection like this was easy, fresh, and new. But one of the facts about affection is that the longer you're with somebody and the more life happens, the more intentional you have to be with expressing affection. You can't let it slide. Because remember, affection is not what a woman wants; it's what she needs.

> **THE LONGER YOU'RE WITH SOMEBODY, THE MORE INTENTIONAL YOU HAVE TO BE WITH AFFECTION.**

With a couple of friendly reminders, I can honestly say, Mike always got back on his game of intentional affection.

A lot of men think, *I didn't grow up being affectionate. I don't know how.* But I encourage you that now is better than never to learn how. Can I get an amen, ladies?

Women Need Communication

We tend to think it's natural for men to talk less than women do. But if you're a husband, you need to stretch yourself in this area if you care about your wife, because she wants to connect with you through words.

And the *kinds* of words your wife needs from you might not be what you think.

Many guys seem to be wired to fix problems. But your wife doesn't always need you to fix whatever problem she is confiding in you. Sometimes she just desires to let you know how she feels or what she's experiencing. What she really wants is for you to empathize and relate.

For example, a wife comes home and she's like, "Oh my goodness, I think this girl Susan is talking about me on my job. I think she said something to Jan, too, because I saw Jan look at me, and I just don't know what to do. Should I confront her?"

In that scenario, most men want to ignore how she felt, belittle the situation, or offer a quick solution. They want to fix it and get it over with. But the wife wants more than that.

Here is something a husband can say to empathize and relate. "I'm sorry that happened to you, sweetheart. I've felt like that before, too." Maybe he can give an example of where he felt like he was being talked about or someone was coming against him.

Men, if you're in the moment and you're kind of like a deer in the headlights, thinking, *How do I relate?* here is a great default statement. You can say, "What can I do to help you in this moment, babe?" I promise you, if you say that, she will give you the answer right there and not be offended. She may say, "I need you to give me a hug and tell me it's gonna be okay." Or she may just need you to be her safe place and listening ear.

Husband, your wife needs communication.

And, wife, your husband has his needs too.

I'm baaaaack! Thanks, Nat!

Not quite yet. I'd like to talk to the ladies too. Remember, I like to communicate.

In Genesis 2:18, when God said, "It is not good for the man to be alone," the first description He gives the woman is "helper." Women, your men need help. And I know some of you just said, "Duh." Seriously, your husband needs you as a helper. He needs your help with some things that only you can give him. My question is, Are you helping him?

Here are some ways he needs you.

Men Need Honor and Respect

These days, this can sound countercultural. We want to react like, "What? You're saying women don't need honor and respect?" Women are independent. They have jobs and make money. They've got more degrees than a thermometer. They deserve honor and respect. All that's true. But still, in a special way of his own, a husband needs honor and respect from his wife.

What does that mean? He needs you to hold him in high regard. He needs you to praise him and speak well of him to others. He needs you to tell him what he does great according to his abilities and his qualities and his achievements.

You might be thinking, *How could I act respectful and honoring when he ain't respectable and honorable?*

Sis, let me give you some ways you can help your hus-

band or your future husband by being respectful and
honoring to him.

1. Allow Him to Fail

A lot of women are damaging their relationships because
they're being mothers instead of partners to their husbands. Men don't want another mother. They don't want
someone to tell them what to do or try to pull them back
from their chosen risk. They want somebody who will
help them achieve their goals.

It reminds me of this one time Mike got a credit card
to buy a huge TV that we really didn't need at the time.
Even though I didn't think it was a smart purchase, I allowed him to make the final decision. That meant I had
to hold my tongue and sacrifice my opinion for the sake of
our unity. One thing I've learned in marriage is to choose
my battles. The TV wasn't worth going into World War III
over.

This purchase actually ended up damaging our credit
and costing a lot of money in interest. But because I allowed Michael to fail without trying to mother him, he
ended up trusting me with his failure by bringing it to me,
and we were able to work on a plan together for the future. I honored my husband by allowing him to make that
decision, and I respected my husband by not belittling him
when it didn't work. Ladies, this is a major key to marriage.

2. Let God Be the Enforcer

If your husband has done something wrong or made a
mistake in your view, then discuss it with him, but don't
feel it's your role to teach him what to do or correct him.
The Holy Spirit convicts and leads.

To all my single and dating ladies, this is why it's so important that the man you're interested in leading you has a relationship with God. You don't want to fight the battles that God can.

And to all my married women, this is why it's so important to pray for your husband. The Bible tells us that the heart of the king is in God's hands and, like water, He can turn it (Proverbs 21:1). He'll do the same thing to the king of your home.

3. Honor the Man You Want Him to Be, Not the Man He Is Right Now

Somebody once told me that you praise what you want repeated. Words of affirmation are one of the strongest ways to communicate your belief in your husband's potential. Take, for instance, Mike and cleaning. He is not the clean-the-whole-house-and-wash-the-dishes-while-I'm-out kind of guy. But when I see him with a broom sweeping, I make sure I tell him, "Boy, I love to see my man cleaning! You do that so well!" Or to encourage him to keep working out, I'll say, "You are so strong. Your muscles look niiiiiiice!"

What many wives don't realize is that they are the prophets in their homes. They can literally speak into existence what's not there, and men will rise to the occasion because they have the belief. That truth leads me into my next major point.

Men Need Support

I heard an older woman once say that if the man is the head, the woman is the neck that supports him. And you can't do nothin' without a neck. Are you supporting your husband emotionally and domestically, with visions for your life and plans for the future?

I've been with Michael for over eighteen years, and I've found that my support is a key ingredient to his success. It doesn't mean that we're doing the same thing. It means that I'm supporting in whatever way that I can. He knows that I have his back, the same way that he has mine. It's hard for anyone to lead, especially a man, knowing that he doesn't have support.

Please don't misunderstand. Being in a support role isn't secondary; it's necessary. It's not a weak role; it takes a tremendous amount of strength. *To support* is to bear all or some of the weight of and to hold up. Here are four ways you can hold up or support your husband:

1. *Presence.* Sometimes just being physically present can be enough for a man to feel truly supported.
2. *Encouragement.* A text message, a word of affirmation, a note in his lunchbox can really spark confidence in your husband.
3. *Wisdom.* You can bring a perspective to a situation that's different than his but can potentially provide support and even solutions for him.
4. *Prayer.* This is my go-to because God made Michael and God knows Michael way more than I do. There are certain things that I will never be able to help with, but God can.

When Michael was a youth pastor, part of his responsibility was to create the stage design for our church. And, y'all, this man had wild ideas with no budget. So, I would support him. I would be present, helping him do whatever I could do. I would encourage him that the design wasn't dumb and it would help people get the message. I would suggest ways to execute our projects efficiently. And, boy, did I pray that we would get finished on time. Looking back now, that was a pattern that I would use to support him from then until now. Contrary to what you've heard, for a wife to support her husband is one of the most sacred things that she can do.

Last but definitely not least . . .

Men Need Sex

Men don't *want* sex; they (say it with me) *need* sex. It's scientifically proven that most men have a more active sex drive than most women. This is not a bad thing. This is actually a good thing or, better yet, a God thing. (See chapter 6, where Mike talks about sex being God's idea.)

And all the men say, "Amen!"

The apostle Paul says,

The husband should fulfill his wife's sexual needs, and the wife should fulfill her husband's needs. The wife gives authority over her body to her husband, and the husband gives authority over his body to his wife.

Do not deprive each other of sexual relations, unless you both agree to refrain from sexual intimacy for a limited time so you can give yourselves more completely to prayer. Afterward, you should come together again so that Satan won't be able to tempt you because of your lack of self-control. (1 Corinthians 7:3–5)

In other words, it's either time to pray or it's time to play!

Wives need sex, too, as Paul says here, but it seems like a lot of them don't need it as much as their husbands. If you're a wife and you've got a healthy sex drive—congratulations! That's great for you. But some other women have to work at it. Sometimes a wife may have to meet her husband's need even if she doesn't necessarily feel like it.

If wives don't meet this need, it leaves a void that men respond to in a variety of ways. Men can get angry. They can feel frustrated. They can feel neglected. A husband can be like, "My wife doesn't even care about me or love me to sacrifice her time or her desires to be able to fulfill this legitimate need."

When this need isn't met, the quality of the marriage goes down and the man starts looking for sex somewhere else. That's not right, but it's real. And we have the ability to safeguard our marriages and relationships as long as we don't confuse wants and needs.

KEY 2: KNOWING HOW TO TALK TO EACH OTHER

We've talked about how women need communication. But actually, men need it, too, even though we may not realize it as clearly. Communication is crucial to a healthy and lasting marriage. And it's not just quantity but also quality. Do we know *how* to communicate?

> **WITH COMMUNICATION, IT'S NOT JUST QUANTITY BUT ALSO QUALITY.**

Speak Each Other's Love Language

Language is an interesting thing. More than seven thousand languages, that we know of, are spoken on the earth today. Everybody can communicate, but not everybody can understand.

I think about a time when Natalie and I were traveling overseas and trying to communicate with someone who spoke a different language. No matter how hard we tried, pointed, slowed down, or enunciated, the look on her face confirmed that this was not working. The frustrations that began to set in were the same frustrations that many marriages face every day. It's like somebody is speaking Mandarin and the other person is speaking French.

We often advise dating couples to read Gary Chapman's *The Five Love Languages*. Married couples should read it too. Chapman describes the love languages of physical touch, quality time, words of affirmation, acts of service, and gifts. He proposes that everyone has a primary way of giving and receiving love. If this interests you, you can take an online quiz to determine your love language.

But let me give you the headline: Chapman's right. Many couples are speaking totally different love languages. They mean well; they just don't know any better. Early on, Natalie and I didn't know any better.

I thought that Natalie liked gifts, but actually her top two love languages are quality time and acts of service. Before I knew this, I would buy Natalie a lot of gifts. Like five pairs of shoes at one time. And she'd be like, "Oh, thank you."

I was like, "I just spent all this money, and all you can say is 'Oh, thank you'?"

She would much rather I spend time with her instead of

YOU ARE LOVED AS IS

God made husbands and wives to meet each other's needs. But the pressure isn't *all* on spouses. In fact, every person needs three things that a spouse can't provide: identity, purpose, and acceptance.

Life tries to label you, but Christ has identified you. Before you're a wife, husband, mommy, daddy, business owner, graduate, daughter, son, or athlete, you had an identity. God says you're called, loved, significant, forgiven, His masterpiece, and His child. Identity can be given only by God. The Bible says that before you were formed in your mother's womb, God knew you.

We believe that purpose is revealed, but purpose is revealed only by the Creator. You don't go to a car mechanic to figure out how your cell phone works. You go to the creator of that product to find the purpose for the creation. In the same way, a relationship cannot give you purpose. It can be a part of purpose, but purpose comes only from the Creator—God.

When Jesus paid the price for humanity's sins, He accepted us as is, like a somewhat damaged but still valuable treasure in a vintage shop. Our shortcomings, our peculiarities, our shining moments—the great things about us and the horrible things about us, and everything in between. Yes, your spouse can learn to love and accept you unconditionally, but God already does.

I am my lover's, and my lover is mine.
(SONG OF SOLOMON 6:3)

spending the money at the store. Don't get me wrong. She likes gifts, just not as much as quality time.

Meanwhile, my top two love languages are physical touch and words of affirmation. On the quiz, you can score 1 through 12. Funny thing is, Natalie's highest score—quality time—is my lowest. She scored a 12 and I scored a 1. That doesn't mean that we aren't supposed to be together. That just means we have to work hard to communicate our love to each other in a way we both receive it.

For Natalie, words of affirmation didn't come naturally, so she had to come up with creative ways to speak that language. She actually checked on Pinterest to learn how to do this. As a result, she got Post-it notes and wrote words of affirmation on them, things like "You can champion your day" and "You are handsome." Then she put them on my mirror in the bathroom so, when I got ready for work, I could read those words that encouraged me, supported me, and affirmed me.

Getting in the habit of speaking each other's love language can be stretching and downright hard, but the work is worth it. It can tremendously transform the satisfaction of your relationship by translating your love into a message that is received and understood.

Know the Power of Your Words

I've alluded to Proverbs 18:21 before about the "power of life and death" being in the tongue (NIV). If you're like me, you've heard that verse many times in your life. But do we really believe that? If we did, we would talk more like Ephesians 4:29 says: "Do not let any unwholesome talk come out of your mouths, but only what is helpful for building others up according to their needs" (NIV).

Hear this statement: Your words are either building up the person you want to be married to or they are tearing down the person you have to be married to. (Don't feel bad if you have to read that twice. Or three times.)

You might be thinking, *I can't use positive language because we have too many problems. We're not getting along.*

You can think of something good to say. Your spouse isn't all wrong. Hold back the critical speech. Find something to praise. It will help your spouse, and it will remind you of the good in the person you chose to marry.

KEY 3: KNOWING HOW TO RESOLVE CONFLICT

Conflict is gonna happen in marriage. It can even be a good thing if it gets differences out in the open and prevents secret resentment. But you don't want to *stay* in conflict. You want to disagree in a way that strengthens your unity without leaving scars.

> **CONFLICT CAN BE A GOOD THING. BUT DON'T *STAY* IN CONFLICT.**

Cut Out Unspoken Expectations

When you don't speak your expectation from the beginning, you are setting up yourself and your spouse to fail. Maybe you feel like your husband or wife already knows what you want—but really, your spouse might not. Then, if you don't voice what you want, it robs the person of the opportunity to actually meet your expectation or your need.

Just after we got married, we were going out on a date. We

didn't have much money then, and we were driving a van without air conditioning. It was really hot that day, and we were talking about it. We decided we would go to QuikTrip to get gas.

We pulled into QuikTrip, and I jumped out to pump the gas. Natalie said, "I'm gonna go get something to drink."

A couple minutes later, Natalie walked out of the QuikTrip with one cup and one doughnut. I couldn't believe it. Although I never asked Natalie to buy me a drink, I'd been sure she would since we'd been talking about how hot it was. And here she was with no drink for me. To make matters worse, her drink was sweet tea—a drink I don't even like. So we couldn't even share the one drink.

When Natalie got back in the car, I was fuming. I watched as she took long sips of her "selfish" tea. It's like I blacked out and the next thing I knew, she took a bite of her doughnut. I grabbed her doughnut and chunked it out the window, then put the van in gear and blew out of the parking lot.

You can imagine the argument. Date night was ruined. Actually, the next two days were ruined, because that's how long it took us to get over being mad at each other.

What really went wrong here was an unspoken expectation. I had never *said* I wanted Natalie to buy me a drink and snack; I had *assumed* she would. Natalie didn't know that because I didn't say it. It was an unspoken expectation.

That's a petty example. But with unspoken expectations, it can get big and serious quickly.

Pay Attention to Your Word Choice and Tone

Another tool to help resolve conflict is to keep your word choice beneficial and leave out the fluff. By this term *fluff*, I mean the secondary emotions. It's the reaction to how you really feel. You're mad. You're frustrated. Okay. But that isn't the real problem or root. And if you speak out of your anger, it might make you feel better but it's not going to resolve the issue. This is hard to do. It's easier to share your secondary emotions than to be vulnerable enough to say what really hurt or even admit that you were hurt at all.

The real problem is what caused you to feel hurt in the first place. You can get to the real problem only by being gentle and humble.

If I'm honest, I was hurt that Natalie didn't get me a drink at QuikTrip because it felt like she didn't care. But it came out in a secondary emotion—anger—and I immaturely heaved that doughnut like I was an NFL quarterback.

Don't yell, "Where was you at on Friday?! Don't you know it's date night? Honestly, it just pissed me off!" That's fluff.

Gently say, "Babe, when date night came on Friday, you forgot and you were hanging out with your friends. It hurt my feelings and made me feel like I wasn't a priority."

The first approach might make you feel better in the moment, but it will create defensiveness and kill your chance to resolve your differences. The second approach sets you up for the results you want. It's all about tone and word choice. Think before you speak.

UNLOCK MARRIAGE SUCCESS

As Michael said in the previous chapter, Satan's plan is to divide and conquer, but God's plan is to unite and conquer. You can get on God's side by pursuing unity at every turn.

A lot of things we have talked about in this chapter (thanks for joining me, Nat!) are useful in all important relationships. They're totally crucial in marriage. To review . . .

- Understand that men and women tend to have different needs. Something that is just a want for one partner might be a need for the other, and the other spouse had better try to meet it or a serious deficit is going to build up in the marriage.
- Make the effort to learn what works best in communication with the partner you married. Convey your love in a way that will be received. Build up; don't tear down.
- Arguments are going to happen, but the more you can do to prevent unnecessary arguments or to bring arguments to a productive conclusion, the less damage your fighting is going to do.

If you're gonna win in marriage, you need these major keys. Make it a top relationship goal to unlock a marriage that helps fulfill the purpose in your life and gives proof to the world that love is possible.

CONCLUSION BULL'S-EYE

As I'm finishing this book, Natalie and I are going to celebrate ten years of marriage. (Cue fireworks.) To you, that might not seem like much. But for us, that is a miracle. It's a miracle because our broken pieces put in God's hand make a masterpiece. It's a relationship that is beautifully flawed, continually worked on, and sealed in sacrifice.

I know you could be thinking, *Will I ever hit the bull's-eye? Are relationship goals even attainable?* And I submit to you that the answer is a resounding yes. But it's a journey, not a destination. Even after a decade of marriage, Natalie and I are still aiming every day at what God has set as the target for our relationship.

You know as well as I do that this book is not the end of your process of learning about relationships. But I do hope it's convinced you to, for the rest of your life, let the Word of God and the Spirit of God lead you as you discover more about how to relate well to people and as you help your friends and loved ones to have better relationships too.

PUT YOUR FAITH WHERE IT BELONGS—IN GOD

Maybe, in the course of reading this book, you have made a life-altering decision. You have decided to try to start a new relationship, or you have decided to end a bad relationship. Or take a break from dating to focus on your relationship with God. Or set some new standards for your behavior before marriage. Or recommit to your marriage. Or resurrect an old dream that you thought had died inside you. Or put your priority back on God.

Whatever it is, I'm proud of you. This is what *Relationship Goals* is all about—your taking aim. And let me assure you—you *can* hit your bull's-eye.

Even if you can't remember how many people you've slept with and still feel horribly alone. Even if bad memories and foolish past associations seem like they'll never let go. Even if you've been divorced three times. Even if you realize that getting rid of all your friends whose bad company is corrupting your good character would leave you completely alone for the time being. Even if you've tried and failed to be faithful to God many times and the thought of trying again just makes you weary. Even then, next time around can be different.

That's because you're not doing this alone. You're not putting your trust in yourself. You're not putting your trust in a friend's or family member's example, like it's some default you have to mindlessly copy.

YOU'RE NOT PUTTING YOUR TRUST IN YOURSELF BUT IN GOD.

You're not putting your trust in a social media profile, dating app, or "how to win friends and influence people" course. You're putting your trust in God.

Remember, as I quoted once before in this book, "God is working in you, giving you the desire and the power to do what pleases him" (Philippians 2:13). I believe that after reading this book, you have the desire. Now He's going to give you the power too. He's going to help you find relationships that will honor Him at the same time they give you more satisfaction and greater fulfillment.

THE TURN

I promised you in chapter 1 that I would keep it real. The truth is that I wrote this book because, unfortunately, I had only one instruction about relationships: "Don't have sex before you're married." That didn't help me at all. I hope *Relationship Goals* will be an asset to you, your friends, your children, your grandchildren, and anybody who wants to be in relationship. I wish somebody would have had this information to give to me. It would have saved me a lot of hurt and a lot of hurting others.

The one thing that I'm a living testimony of is God's grace. Even though I messed up, He worked it into His plan. Romans 8:28 says, "We know that God causes everything to work together for the good of those who love God and are called according to his purpose for them." It doesn't matter what your current relationship status is—there is hope for you. Our hope is found in Jesus. And let me tell you a secret: He wants your relationships to work more than you do.

So, as you take aim, remember it's about progression, not perfection. You will make mistakes. You will make poor relational choices. You will even at times sin. But thank God for Jesus, because where sin abounds, grace abounds much more (Romans 5:20, NKJV).

In this season of life, I go to a lot of weddings, and there's a very popular line dance called the Wobble. If you've never seen this dance, it's basically a back-and-forth movement following a call-and-response from the DJ. But one part of this dance is vital to everything: the turn. It never fails; at every wedding, someone doesn't get the turn.

Okay, what does the turn have to do with relationship goals?

Just like the dance, this is also the pivotal part in your relationship journey with Christ: the turn.

Acts 3:19 says, "Now repent of your sins and turn to God, so that your sins may be wiped away." Many people are stuck in the back-and-forth of relationships. The back-and-forth of cycles. The back-and-forth of sexual purity. The back-and-forth of unhealthy relationships. The back-and-forth of giving in to temptation. The back-and-forth of discontentment. But they forget to turn. Repenting is just turning. It's turning from something and turning to something. I'm not sure what you're turning from, but I know who you need to turn to. It's Jesus.

> I'M NOT SURE WHAT YOU'RE TURNING FROM, BUT I KNOW WHO YOU NEED TO TURN TO. JESUS.

The blessing of turning is what the scripture goes on to say: "Then times of refreshment will come from the presence of the Lord" (verse 20). And that's what I'm praying for your relationships—that your relationships will be refreshed. Your dating relationships will be refreshed. Your marriage relationship will be refreshed. Your love for yourself will be refreshed. Your business relationships will be refreshed. Your family relationships will be refreshed. I think y'all get it. I pray that all your relationships will be refreshed.

So, don't get stuck in the back-and-forth. Learn to turn. It's your season to win in relationships.

ACKNOWLEDGMENTS

Every accomplishment in my life has been supported in love and prayer by some very important people, and this book is no exception. I have been blessed to be surrounded by a host of people that uplift, execute, and believe in the vision that God has given to me. I would like to take this time to acknowledge my community, my team, and my family.

To my wife, and so much more, Natalie Diane Todd, your love for me is inconceivable. Thank you for never giving up on me through my deficiencies, insecurity, and immaturity. Your prayers, grace, and patience allowed me to grow into the man I am today. Thank you for our children, Isabella, Michael Jr., and Ava; they bring so much bliss into my life. You affirm me and encourage me, and you push me beyond my comprehension of success. You will forever be my partner, my passion, and my purpose.

To my parents, Tommy (aka "The Captain") and Brenda Todd, thank you for your abounding wisdom and relentless belief in me. Your encouragement, prayers, and example of faith have shaped me into the man I am today. Thank you for showing me how to lead my family with unconditional love, abundant grace, and strength. Thank you for being the greatest depiction of our heavenly Father's love here on this earth.

To my brother, Brentom Todd, thank you for being undoubtedly willing to do whatever it takes to ensure my health, success, and sustainability. You stepped outside of your brotherly role in my life and cared for me as a friend. Without your commitment, resilience, and determination, I couldn't do what I do today. I love you, bro.

To Brie and Aaron Davis, the friends turned sister/brother I never knew I needed, thank you for always being right by my side. Thank you for your persistent authenticity in our friendship. Through every failed project and successful venture, you both have remained a consistent support system. Thank you for taking this journey with me and being everything I've ever needed you to be. And thank you for letting me use your house as my personal book-writing office.

To Amber Guipttons, my executive assistant extraordinaire, thank you for keeping my life and family so excellently structured. No task is ever too big and no problem unsolvable. Your commitment to our family empowers us to live a life filled with balance and vast excitement. We look forward to many more memorable milestones with you by our side.

To Trey Thaxton and Jonathan Vinnett, thank you for illustrating the visions of my heart with such clarity. For years you have made my words come to life and illuminated the ideas that I couldn't always adequately articulate. Your ability to see beyond the tangible has afforded me the privilege to create in confidence so that my vision would be accurately interpreted to the world. Thank you for growing with me on this ever-evolving journey of creativity.

To Alex Fields, my literary agent, thank you for playing an instrumental role in making this dream come true. Thank you for your guidance, support, and confidence in the process of this project. You've been by my side every step of the way, sharing your wisdom, giving guidance, and lending encouragement whenever necessary. Thank you for believing in the vision that was given to me; thank you for believing in me.

To Eric Stanford, thank you for your many contributions to this project. In a great way, without you, this would not be possible. Your competence in the literary sphere has ensured that this book would be created and interpreted in excellence. Thank you for taking the time to share this experience with me and making it one I will never forget.

To Melody Dunlap, my God-sister and good friend, thank you for using your vast array of talents to hoist any project I've asked you to partner with me on. From adolescence to adulthood, you've been my go-to executor for all of my wild and innovative ideas. Thank you for continuing this journey with me.

To the couples whose stories are depicted across the pages of this book, thank you for your transparency, vulnerability, and enduring selflessness. Your commitment to everlasting healing and restoration will bring just that and so much more to the lives of those who consume this project. Thank you for your trust in me, allowing me to guide you to a place of solace and redemption.

To the team at WaterBrook, thank you for your commitment to the execution and completion of this project. The joy, excitement, and energy that you all brought made this an unforgettably enjoyable experience. Your attention to detail and focus on even the small things left me confident that I was working with the right team. All of your hard work and efforts are very much appreciated.

To Transformation Church and TC Nation, this is for you!

Thank you for your love, support, and prayers for me and my family. The relentless affection that I feel from you motivates me to continue the fulfillment of my purpose.

To the TC staff, thank you all for your continued dedication and commitment to the vision and partners of TC. Thank you for allowing me to re-present God outside the walls of our church. I'm humbled and honored to be your leader.

ABOUT THE AUTHOR

MICHAEL TODD is the lead pastor of Transformation Church in Tulsa, Oklahoma, alongside his wife, Natalie. They were entrusted with Transformation Church from the founding pastor, Bishop Gary McIntosh, in 2015, after fifteen years of operation.

Their personal philosophy and driving passion at Transformation Church is re-presenting God to the lost and found for transformation in Christ. They aspire to reach their community, city, and world with the gospel presented in a relevant and progressive way. The fast-growing church publishes a magazine called *Transpire,* produces their own worship music, Transformation Worship, and hosted the first Transformation Conference in fall 2019. You can find out more details about Transformation Church at www.transformchurch.us.

In addition, Michael has spoken at a variety of influential churches, events, universities, and conferences, including Elevation Church (Steven Furtick), C3 Conference (Fellowship Church), Lakewood Church (Joel Osteen), VOUS Conference (VOUS Church), Relentless Church (John Gray), XO Conference (Gateway Church), and others.

Michael and Natalie have been married since 2010 and live in Tulsa with three beautiful children—their daughters, Isabella and Ava, and their son, Michael Jr.

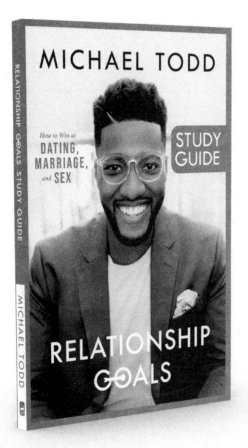

Study Guide Also Available!
IAmMikeTodd.com/Relationship-Goals